THE NAPOLEONIC WARS I

ARMS and UNIFORMS

Other titles in this series:

The Napoleonic Wars Part II

Arms and Uniforms I–Ancient Egypt to the 18th Century

Arms and Uniforms II–18th Century to the Present Day

Liliane and Fred Funcken

THE NAPOLEONIC WARS

PART I

The French, British, Prussian and Spanish armies

WARD LOCK LIMITED · LONDON

ISBN 0 7063 1406 9

First published in Great Britain 1973 by
Ward Lock Limited, 116 Baker Street,
London, W1M 2BB

Designed by Conal A. Buck

Text filmset in 12/16pt Baskerville
by V. Siviter Smith & Co Ltd

Printed and bound by Casterman S.A.
Tournai, Belgium

Contents

Introductory Note

In the section dealing with the French Army, we have, in general, retained the French titles for the various ranks. The organisation of the French Army was different from that of the British Army so that, although the actual words can be translated, their meaning is not necessarily the same. Thus in the British Army, except in the Foot Guards, a Major was the second-in-command of a battalion whereas in the French Army, the equivalent rank, *chef de bataillon,* commanded the battalion and the title 'major' was not applied to him. Similarly the *maréchal de camp,* later called a *général de brigade,* was not the same as a Brigadier-General or a Brigadier.

Likewise in most cases we have retained the actual names of the regiments and corps as to transpose them into English merely makes them look grotesque without conveying any greater meaning. Some, too, cannot be translated. A good example is what the Germans called a *Leib-Regiment,* which in straight translation becomes 'Body Regiment'. What the term actually means, however, is a Regiment of which the Colonel is the King. To twist this into 'The King's' or 'The King's Own' does not produce a satisfactory answer, for the significance, in English, is entirely different. We still have 'King's' Regiments in the British Army to-day, although our Monarch is a Queen.

THE FRENCH ARMY

Napoleon and his staff

On 18 May 1804, Napoleon Bonaparte received the Senate who had come to proclaim him Emperor of the French 'for the glory and for the good of the Republic'. Ten years before, this man had been an ordinary Gunner Captain!

Napoleon Bonaparte was born on 15 August 1769 at Ajaccio, on the Island of Corsica which had been annexed by France just a year earlier.[1] The quarrelsome little boy, who roved among the wild rocks of his native island, had only shown an interest in mathematics. In due course, however, he was sent to France, his fatherland, to be trained as an Officer of the King. In 1784, he entered the *École de Mars* as a Gentleman Cadet, and, at sixteen, he became a Second Lieutenant in the Regiment of La Fère. He was twice wounded during the siege of Toulon, in 1793, where he drove out the British, and was promoted *général de brigade* on the recommendation of the Commander of the Forces there. This officer, an unwitting prophet, wrote to the Committee of Public Safety, 'Reward and promote this young man, for, if we neglect him, he will promote himself.'

1. Having purchased the island from the Genoese Republic, Louis XV proclaimed the union of Corsica with France on 15 August 1768. Two expeditions were required to crush the resistance of the Corsicans (Ponte Nuovo 9 May 1769) and put the union into effect.

1. Aide-de-camp, 1804.
2. Marshal, undress uniform.
3. *Général de division*, 1805.
4. Marshal, plain coat.
5. *Général de brigade*, frock coat, 1805.
6. Marshal of the Empire, 1804.
7. Murat, when Governor-General of Paris, 1804.
8. The Emperor, 1804.
9. *Général de brigade*, 1804.

7
8
9
1
2
3
4
5
F. FUNCKEN.

And he did promote himself with meteoric rapidity: *général de division* and Commander-in-Chief of the Army of the Interior at twenty-six, in 1796 he was appointed *général en chef* and given command of the Army of Italy where he was to 'conquer the most beautiful lands in Europe'; next Egypt; then the *coup d'état* of 18 Brumaire (9 November 1799) when he became First Consul; in 1802, after the Treaties of Lunéville and Amiens, he made himself Consul for life and finally, in 1804, he crowned himself Emperor of France. After this astounding rise to power, France gave herself heart and soul to this extraordinary man who had brought her so much glory.

The Empire, in its turn, gave birth to a military aristocracy that was to raise the prestige of Imperial France to the level she had enjoyed under the *ancien régime*.

Philip II Auguste had created the first Marshal of France in 1185, but the Republic abolished the honour. Napoleon reinstituted it by a decree dated 19 May 1804 when he appointed fourteen of his old companions in arms, who had helped him to power, Marshals of the Empire. Their average age was forty and their names were: Augereau (1757–1816), Bernadotte (1763–1844), Berthier (1753–1815), Bessières (1768–1813), Brune (1763–1815), Davout (1770–1823), Jourdan (1762–1833), Lannes (1769–1809), Masséna (1756–1817), Moncey (1754–1842), Mortier (1768–1835), Murat (1767–1815), Ney (1769–1815) and Soult (1769–1851).

1. Aide-de-camp (Colonel) to a *Général d'armée*, 1807.
2. Aide-de-camp (Captain) to a *Général de brigade*, 1805.
3. Colonel on the Staff, 1805.
4. Regimental Adjutant.
5. Aide-de-camp to a *Général d'armée*, 1805.
6. Murat, 1805.
7. The Emperor, 1805.
8. Marshal of the Empire, 1805.

1
2
3
4
5
6
7
8
F. FUNCKEN.

Their numbers were raised to eighteen by the creation, in 1804, of four honorary Marshals, and further additions were made in succeeding years: Victor (1766–1841) in 1807; Oudinot (1767–1847), Macdonald (1765–1840) and Marmont (1774–1852) in 1809; Suchet (1772–1826) in 1811; Gouvion-Saint-Cyr (1764–1830) in 1812; Poniatowski (1762–1813) in 1813 and Grouchy (1766–1847) in 1815.

The number of general officers was also considerably increased, there were 259 promotions to *général de division* and 703 to *général de brigade* between 1805 and 1815.

All the same, this distinguished company, who yearly paid a heavier price as they led younger and more inexperienced men into battle, were treated by the Emperor with a suspicion and a disdain that bordered on contempt. 'Generals count for nothing,' said Napoleon, and he treated his Marshals, from whom he demanded a blind obedience, no better. 'Only I know what I should do,' was his summing up of the situation. With a few exceptions, the military leaders of the Empire knuckled-under, with sickening

1. Colonel on the Staff, Imperial Headquarters, 1809.
2. Personal Servants, Imperial Household.

3, 4. Aides-de-camp to Marshal Berthier.

5. The Emperor's Telescope-bearer.
6. Murat, King of Naples, 1810.
7. Berthier.
8. The Emperor, 1809.
9. Roustan, the Emperor's Mameluke Personal Servant.
10. Chief of Staff, 1809.
11. *Général de division*, 1809.

11
10
9
8
7
6
5
1
2
3
4
FUNCKEN.

servility in some cases. Rivalries, springing mostly from earlier quarrels, set the Marshals against each other, blinding them to realities so much that they brought disasters on themselves by refusing to help each other in time of need. This was especially so in Spain, Portugal and Russia, where they were not immediately under their master's eye.

Despite their glory and fame, there were too many of the marshals for them to give way to the lure of gain, notwithstanding the encouragement of their emperor who believed by a rather dubious generalisation, that greed and ambition were the surest guarantees of their loyalty to himself. However, surfeited by the goods of this world, most of the Marshals who were sickened by the whole affair, withdrew from the man who had made their fortunes.

These men, of whom we have drawn a rather poor picture, nevertheless had one quality in common, their extraordinary courage, and it was this that brought the French Army its lasting glory.

1. *Général de division*, 1812.
2. Marshal, 1812.
3. *Général de division*, 1812.
4. *Général de brigade*, wearing cloak, 1815.
5. General Officer, 1812.
6. Aide-de-camp, undress, 1813.
7. *Général de division*, 1813.
8. Surgeon, Imperial Headquarters.
9. Survey Department, 1810.
10. Murat, 1812.

7
8
9
10
6
1
2
3
4
5
& F. FUNCKEN.

The Emperor devised the most elaborate uniforms for his Marshals and for the General Officers, but this extravagance of gold lace and embroidery stopped sharply there. Dressed more simply, the *adjudants généraux* or *adjudants-commandants* were employed as Chiefs of Staff. Next came the *Aides-de-Camp* to the General Officers, of whom a Marshal had six, a *général de division* had three, and a *général de brigade* had two. Like most extra-regimentally employed officers, the *aides-de-camp* seldom wore the regulation dress, preferring confections of their own devising.

A certain number of young officers were chosen from the different arms of the Service to act as couriers for the Emperor. They belonged to the Household and were limited to twelve in all; they enjoyed the title of *Officier d'Ordonnance*. Their uniform was light blue, embroidered in silver. Napoleon rewarded their services by returning them to regimental duty in one rank higher than that they had held whilst on his personal staff.

1. Aide-de-camp to Marshal Berthier, 1809.
2. Aide-de-camp to Marshal Bernadotte, 1807.
3. Aide-de-camp to a Marshal, full dress, 1807.
4. Aide-de-camp to Murat.
5. Aide-de-camp to a General Officer.
6. Aide-de-camp to a General Officer, 1810.
7. Aide-de-camp to a *Général de division*, 1812.

7
6
5
1
2
3
4
FUNCKEN.

Drum-Majors and Musicians

The musicians' rôle was not restricted to the ceremonial parades, because Napoleon, who generally had little interest in music, realised its importance to the soldiers and to the general public. Apart from the regulation bugle and drum calls, such as Reville and Lights Out, the tunes played by the military bands were often popular songs; the old Republican airs which had been the favourites of the masses, aroused the Emperor's suspicions as he considered them too revolutionary. So it was that the troops marched past to the strains of '*J'aime l'oignon frit à l'huile*', a song from the latest musical, and the Bandmasters set about arranging suitable popular tunes as marches.

David Buhl, the best trumpet-player of his day, trained more than six hundred musicians at the school at Versailles, and his methods, which were widely adopted, were regarded as classic for many years.

DRUM-MAJORS

1. Infantry of the Line, 1812–14.
2. Infantry of the Line, undress, 1812.
3. Light Infantry, 1809.
4. 3rd Regiment of the Line, 1810.
5. 29th Regiment of the Line, 1807.
6. Infantry of the Line, 1807.

6
5
1
2
3
4
FUNCKEN.

Following the principles of Fétis,[2] a band was made up basically of six to eight ordinary clarinets, one Eb clarinet, one piccolo, two horns, two bassoons, a trumpet, two or three trombones, one or two serpents, a bass drum, cymbals, a side-drum and a Jingling Johnnie (or Chinese pavilion).

The Bandmasters quickly set about composing numerous quick and slow marches. One of them, a certain Gebauer who was held to have composed many of the best marches of the time, perished along with the rest of his Band during the Russian Campaign.

Originally, the musicians wore blue coats without lapels and hats trimmed with gold but, after 1806, their dress became more elaborate. In action, the musicians were used as ammunition carriers and as stretcher-bearers. In the Light Infantry, the bugles, fifes, and drums had an equally important rôle.

2. François-Joseph Fétis (1784–1871), Belgian composer and musician.

BANDS AND DRUMS

1. 1808.
2. Bass Drummer, 1812.
3. Light Infantry, 1812.
4. Bandmaster, 1812.
5. Bandmaster, 1809.
6. 1809.
7. 1812.
8, 9. Light Infantry, 1812.
10. Bandmaster, 1805.
11. Bandmaster, 1809.

8
9
10
11
6
7
1
2
3
4
5
FUNCKEN.

The virtuosity of the drummers was quite remarkable. The famous *Batterie d'Austerlitz*, with its variations in rhythms and the differences of sound made by striking the drum on the skin or the hoop, produced what is almost a sonata for the drums. The difficulties inherent in its performance rule out the suggestion that the piece was played at the battle of which it bears the name.

The drummers were often very brave men, and they were generally the first to come in contact with the enemy. They were trained by the Drum-Major whose staff was originally a simple cane used to chastise his turbulent subordinates. Under the Empire, the dress of the drummers went to all extremes, so that they looked like fairground clowns. By an order of 1812, bandsmen, fifes, drums and drum-majors adopted a green uniform. This was the well-known Imperial livery, decorated with lace showing the Imperial Cypher 'N' and the Eagle.

STAFF BANDS

1. Jingling Johnnie.
2. Clarinet.
3. Serpent.
4. Bassoon.
8. French horn.
5–7, 9, and 10. Other bandsmen.

9
10
7
8
5
6
1
2
3
4

The Infantry

An army of 200,000 intended for the invasion of England had been assembled in camps along the Channel coast. It was a first-class force, one of the best that had ever been perhaps. Inspired by an unshakeable faith in their leader the *Petit Tondu* (Little Shavenpate–the soldiers' nickname for Napoleon); the Army of England, as it was known, underwent intensive training for so long that the men were becoming stale. The defeat of Admiral de Villeneuve at Trafalgar in 1805 obliged Napoleon to abandon the idea of invading England, and the army that had been assembled on the coast became the Grand Army. It was this army that, starting with the Battle of Austerlitz on 2 December 1805, enjoyed an uninterrupted series of victories; Jena and Auerstadt in 1806 and Eylau and Friedland in East Prussia in 1807, when the Peace of Tilsit was concluded.

More than half the men in 1805 had served during the wars of the Revolution and of the Consulate. They still wore the two-cornered cocked hat of the Revolution and the long-skirted tail-coat of blue with white lapels.

The demi-brigade of the Revolutionary period had been replaced by the regiment which consisted of two to eight battalions, each sub-divided into companies.

In battle, the line companies were drawn up in the centre (for which reason they were known as the centre companies), with the grenadier company on the right flank and the light infantry company on the left flank (hence, these were called the flank companies). In light infantry regiments, the grenadier company was replaced by a carabinier company. A brigade consisted of two or three regiments, and a division of two brigades. The role of the flank companies was clearly defined. The light infantry, who were small and agile, spread themselves out and harassed the opposing infantry with

LIGHT INFANTRY I

1. Rifleman, 10th Regiment.
2. Light Infantryman, 10th Regiment.
3. Carabinier, 8th Regiment, marching order, 1809.
4. Sergeant, Carabinier Company, 8th Regiment, 1809.
5. Drummer, 17th Regiment, 1809.
6. Rifleman, 1804–6.
7. Officer, Rifles, 1810.
8. Carabinier, 1810.
9. Pioneer, serving in Spain.
10. Sergeant-Major, serving in Spain.
11. Carabinier.
12. Cornet-player, Light Infantry.

11
12
9
10
8
7
6
4
2
1
5
3
FUNCKEN.

individual, well-aimed fire. The grenadiers, big men, were supposed to urge on the centre companies and keep them in the firing line.

Apart from certain details, the uniform and arms (a short musket, called a fusil notably), there was no practical difference between the light infantry regiments and those of the line. They fought side by side and each shared the other's glory.

The greatest enemy of the infantry was the cavalry, which, if it could fall upon a unit of infantry in open order, had no difficulty in breaking it up and cutting it to pieces. The defence was found in the square. During this period, squares were generally formed on the battalion, for this proved the quickest and simplest method. The flank companies held the corners and filled the inside of the square, while the centre companies with their wall of bayonets formed the sides. When attacking, the infantry advanced in column by divisions, a formation from which it was easy to deploy into line or to form the square.

Despite their successes in battle, the infantry's arms left much to be desired. Their principal weapon, the musket, was a pattern introduced in 1777 and was still second-rate, despite various modifications. Moreover, it was out-classed by the muskets of the opposing armies, so that the French soldiers armed themselves with enemy weapons picked up on the battlefield.

The French flintlock weighed 10 lbs and was 5 ft long. It was accurate up to about ten yards, but was hopelessly inadequate over two hundred yards. The 0.67 in. ball was spherical and was contained with the powder charge in a sealed paper cartridge which had to be bitten open so that the powder could be poured into the barrel. The paper was then used as a wad, which was driven home with the ramrod. Next, the ball was rammed in, finally, the priming-charge had to be put in the pan. The operation took twelve movements and a minute to perform.

INFANTRY OF THE LINE I
(over page)

1. Private, Battalion Company, full dress, 1804–7.
2. Light Infantryman, service dress, 1806.
3. Private, Battalion Company, 1805.
4. Colonel.
5. Light Infantryman.
6. Fife, 1805.
7. Grenadier.
8. Grenadier, marching order.
9. Cornet-player, Light Infantry.
10. Pioneer, 1805.
11. Lieutenant, Grenadier Company, 1805.
12. Private, Battalion Company, service dress, 1805.

LIGHT INFANTRY II

1. Drummer, Carabiniers, 1812.
2. Chasseur, 10th Light Infantry, 1812.
3. Light Infantryman, 5th Regiment.
4. Pioneer, 1810–12.
5. Chasseur, 1812.
6. Field Officer, 1812.
7. Carabinier, 5th Regiment.
8. Light Infantryman, 3rd Regiment, 1814–15.
9. Officer, Chasseurs.
10. Chasseur, marching order, 1812.
11. Private, Battalion Company, marching order, 1812.

7
8
5
6
4
9
10
11
3
2
1
FUNCKEN

4
3
5
1
2
L. & F.
FUNCKEN

10
11
12
7
8
9

Even then, the musket would not necessarily go off, for misfires were quite frequent. These defects, coupled with the natural hastiness of the French soldier, led to his relying mainly on his bayonet. This was triangular in section and nearly 16 in. long, but it was not particularly strong. Each man carried fifty rounds and three spare flints. In addition to the bayonet, he had a short, curved sword, called a *briquet*.

In 1804, the light infantry wore the blue coatee introduced in 1799 with scarlet lapels and facings, and waistcoat and breeches of the same colour. The shako, Hungarian in origin, which the light infantry had been the first to adopt, bore a brass plate in the form of a hunting horn. The carabinier company had a red festoon on the shako. The light infantry did not have drums at this time, but used the horn with its characteristically sharp tone. The carabinier company and the centre companies were distinguished by their red collars, the light infantry company had yellow collars.

In 1812, the red collars of the flank companies and the centre companies were piped with blue, and the cuffs, facings, and turn-backs became blue with white piping. The carabinier company had a grenade badge on their turn-backs; the centre companies had a white hunting horn and the light infantry company had a buff hunting horn. Their breeches were white. The epaulettes were scarlet piped with red for the carabinier company, blue piped with white for the line companies, and buff piped with blue for the light infantry company. Departures from the regulation uniform were common: plumes appeared on the shakos, and the patterns of the helmet plates followed the whim of the Colonel. Throughout this period, the officers wore the long tail coat.

There were 37 light infantry regiments in 1804, but five of them existed on paper only, the idea being to deceive the enemy about the real strength of the army.

INFANTRY OF THE LINE II

1. Grenadier, full dress, 1807.
2. Private, Battalion Company, 1807.
3. Light Infantryman, 1806–7.
4. Sergeant-Major, Grenadier Company, 1806–7.
5. Grenadier, 1806–7.

2
3
1
4
5

In the early days of the Empire, the infantry of the line retained the uniform worn in the Revolutionary Wars. Now, the hat was replaced by the shako with a brass plate and a cockade. This headdress was made up of a felt body with a leather crown. There was a buckle at the back which allowed the head-band to be adjusted to the size of the wearer. There was a leather peak in front and a plate above this, the form of which varied at different times, surmounted by a cockade. A plume, or a tuft, was inserted behind the cockade. A white festoon, fastened on either side of the crown, encircled the shako and ended in tassels on the right. The shako was fitted with a brass scaled chin-strap. Besides being a good protection against sword-cuts, the shako proved useful for carrying all kinds of odd things: apples, combs, onions, blacking, a mirror and even the odd bottle or two.

In 1806, the greatcoat was introduced and the white coatee replaced the blue one because of the shortage of indigo dye. Only a few regiments were re-clothed, but this did not prevent those that were from making modifications of their own, despite the clearly-worded regulations. The 3rd, 4th, 8th, 12th, 14th, 15th, 17th, 18th, 19th, 21st, 22nd, 24th, 25th, 27th, 28th, 33rd, 34th, and 86th Regiments of Infantry were selected to receive the new dress immediately, it consisted of a cloth coatee and waistcoat, stockinette breeches and a drab cloth greatcoat.

The regiments, as a whole, were divided into fourteen series of eight regiments. In each series, the first four regiments had brass buttons and horizontal side-pockets, and the other four had white-metal buttons and vertical side-pockets.

Within each series, the distinguishing colours were worn:

1st and 5th Regiments–on the lapels, cuffs and collar
2nd and 6th Regiments–on the lapels and cuffs
3rd and 7th Regiments–on the lapels and collar
4th and 8th Regiments–on the cuffs and collar

INFANTRY OF THE LINE III

1. Private, Grenadier Company, 1808.
2, 3. Privates, Light Infantry Company, 1808.
4. Private, Battalion Company, 1809.
5. Grenadier, 1809.
6. Light Infantryman, winter dress, 1809–10.
7. Private, Battalion Company, 1807.
8. Drummer, Battalion Company, 1809.
9–11. Shakos, 1804, 1806, and 1810.

8
9
10
11
7
4
5
2
1
3

The distinguishing colours of the series were:

SERIES		REGIMENTS		COLOUR	
SERIES	1	REGIMENTS	1–8	COLOUR	Imperial Green
	2		9–16		Black
	3		17–24		Scarlet
	4		25–32		Deep Yellow
	5		33–40		Violet
	6		41–48		Sky Blue
	7		49–56		Pink
	8		57–64		Saffron
	9		65–72		Dark Blue
	10		73–80		Pale Yellow
	11		81–88		Grass Green
	12		89–96		Maroon
	13		97–104		Crimson
	14		105–112		Iron Grey

A substitute for indigo was soon found in the native French plant, woad, and the orders were cancelled in 1807.

In 1812, the infantry of the line received a new pattern of coatee,[3] which buttoned down to the waist, concealing the waistcoat. The skirt was shortened to about 9 in. The grenadier company and the centre companies had scarlet collars with blue piping, and the light infantry company had buff collars. The white lapels were piped with scarlet, and the cuffs were scarlet piped with white, with blue slashes piped with scarlet. The vertical side-pockets were piped with scarlet. The white turn-backs, piped with white, bore the crowned letter 'N' in blue for the centre companies, a red grenade for the grenadier company, and a buff hunting horn for the light infantry company.

The shoulder-straps were blue with red edges for the centre companies, scarlet with blue edges for the grenadier company, and buff with blue edges for the light infantry company. The gaiters, too, had been shortened and now came only up to the knee.

3. This ruling did not apply to the *Garde Impériale*, which formed a separate wing (see Volume II).

INFANTRY OF THE LINE IV

1. Ensign, 1815.
2. Non-Commissioned officer of Colour Party, 1812.
3. Private, Battalion Company, 1812–14.
4. Corporal, Grenadier Company, in marching order, 1812.
5. Corporal, Light Infantry Company, 1812–14.
6. Company Officer, 1812.
7. *Porte-fanion*, 1812.
8. Transport Officer, 1813.
9. Private, Light Infantry Company, 1814.
10. Private, Grenadier Company, 1813.

7
8
9
5
6
10
4
1
2
3
F.FUNCKEN.

The shako of the centre companies and the light infantry company was of the same pattern, but the latter had a yellow plume with yellow chevrons on the sides. The shako of the grenadier company was taller, of the cavalry style, and had a red plume and red chevrons. The light infantry companies wore a dark green tuft in the 1st company, a sky blue tuft in the 2nd, a deep yellow tuft in the 3rd, and a violet tuft in the 4th company.

In the early days of the Empire, the foot soldier wore his hair *en queue,* save a few who had been shorn *à la Titus* in imitation of Napoleon whose hair-style had earned him the nickname of *le Petit Tondu.* Some had grown pigtails of an astounding length and were very proud of them, but now these fell to the barber's scissors.

In 1813, there were 156 regiments in the infantry of the line, but twenty-one of them were notional for reasons that we have already explained.

At the head of each regiment, there marched the pioneers wearing bearskins and white leather aprons. With axes on their shoulders, the pioneers led the parade, followed by the drum-major and the band and drums. This group captured the imagination of the Colonels who, regardless of any orders there might be on the subject, strove to outdo each other in producing the most spectacular display.

Following the triumphs of the Grand Army, the hastily-assembled forces of 1809 endured a succession of defeats in Spain, and that was followed by the Army of the Twenty Nations which was destroyed in Russia. Last came the army of 1813, gallant but too weak to stand up to the assembled strength of the Allies.

INFANTRY OF THE LINE V

1, 2. Shako plates, Light Infantry, 1807–12.
3–5. Skirt ornaments, Grenadier, Light Infantry, and Battalion Companies, 1812.
6, 7. Shako plates, Infantry of the Line, 1810 and 1812.
8, 9. Musket and bayonet, pattern 1801.
10. Private, Battalion Company, 1814.
11. Private, Grenadier Company, 1814.
12. Private, Light Infantry Company, 1814.
13. Private, Battalion Company, 1813–14.

1
2
3
4
5
6
7
10
11
12
13
8
9

Regimental Artillery

At the time of the Revolution, each battalion of infantry had been given four guns, but this number was halved in 1795. Then, in 1803, despite the objections raised by the infantry, they were withdrawn as being of little use.

In 1809, each regiment in the Corps commanded by Davout, Masséna, and Oudinot was given two guns, 3 pounders or 5 pounders captured from the Austrians, together with 150 to 200 rounds. The guns were manned by the regiment, and the officers and men vied with each other to serve in the gun detachments, who were given a distinctive uniform. The regimental artillery was short-lived and was abolished in 1813.

REGIMENTAL ARTILLERY AND OFFICERS OF THE INFANTRY OF THE LINE

1. Officer, stable jacket, 1807.
2. Company Officer, Grenadier Company, 1812.
3. Artillery Driver, 1811.
4. Gunner, 1811.
5. Gunner, full dress, 1811.
6. Subaltern, Battalion Company, 1809–12.
7. Subaltern, Light Infantry Company, 1809.
8. Artillery Driver, marching order, 1811.
9. Austrian 3 pounder Gun.

7
8
6
5
1
2
3
4

The Cavalry

The imperial cavalry was divided into heavy cavalry (cuirassiers and carabiniers), cavalry of the line (dragoons and lancers), and light cavalry (hussars and *chasseurs à cheval*).

CUIRASSIERS I

1. 13th Regiment, 1809.
2. 11th Regiment, 1804–6.
3. Stable dress, 1804.
4. Trumpeter, 8th Regiment, 1804–12.
5. Field Officer, 7th Regiment, 1809.
6. Subaltern, undress, 1806.
7. Trumpeter, 12th Regiment, 1804–12.

Cuirassiers

In 1804, there were twelve regiments of cuirassiers. As they specialised in the charge, they were protected by bullet-proof helmets and cuirasses. The cuirass was made of wrought steel, and consisted of a breast and back plate, the two being connected by brass shoulder straps and a strap round the waist. The helmet was of steel, similar to that of the dragoons, and surmounted with a brass crest decorated with a tuft and a black mane. The skull was wrapped with a turban of black fur and there was a scarlet plume on the left side. There were several different patterns of helmet and of cuirass, and their quality declined with the Empire.

The cuirass was lined to prevent its wearing out the coatee, the lining was of crimson cloth edged with white.

The regiments had the following distinguishing colours:

	COLLAR	PIPING ON COLLAR	FACINGS	CUFF-SLASHES	PIPING ON CUFF-SLASHES	TURNBACKS
1st	Scarlet	Blue	Scarlet	Scarlet		Scarlet
2nd	Scarlet	Blue	Scarlet	Blue	Scarlet	Scarlet
3rd	Scarlet	Blue	Blue	Scarlet	Scarlet	Scarlet
4th	Saffron	Blue	Saffron	Saffron		Saffron
5th	Saffron	Blue	Saffron	Blue	Saffron	Saffron
6th	Saffron	Blue	Blue	Saffron	Saffron	Saffron
7th	Pale Yellow	Blue	Pale Yellow	Pale Yellow		Pale Yellow
8th	Pale Yellow	Blue	Pale Yellow	Blue	Pale Yellow	Pale Yellow
9th	Pale Yellow	Blue	Blue	Pale Yellow	Pale Yellow	Pale Yellow
10th	Pink	Blue	Pink	Pink		Pink
11th	Pink	Blue	Pink	Blue	Pink	Pink
12th	Pink	Blue	Blue	Pink	Pink	Pink

7
6
5
1
2
4
3
F. Funcken

In addition to a straight sabre, the cuirassiers carried two pistols, and after 1812, a short musket and bayonet. Underneath the cuirass, they wore a royal blue coatee, with turnback badges in the form of blue grenades. The pockets were vertical, and the epaulettes had scarlet fringes.

The cuirassiers, nicknamed the 'Big Brothers', were the finest cavalry troops of the Empire. The earth shook beneath the fury of their charges. At Montmirail in 1814, they slaughtered a third of a Russian force of thirty-thousand in one charge, and at Waterloo they fought to the death.

The same distinguishing colours were still used in 1812, while those of the 13th and 14th Regiments, raised in 1809, were: 13th collar and turnbacks, and cuffs, blue-grey; cuff-slashes, blue. 14th the same except the cuff-slashes which were blue-grey.

The horse furniture consisted of a shabracque (saddle-cloth), holster-caps, and a valise, all of which were blue laced with white. In 1812, the regimental number was shown in white on the valise.

In the earlier days, the trumpeters wore various fantastic uniforms, but they adopted the imperial livery in 1812, with neither cuirass nor pouch. All cavalry wore buckskin breeches and thigh-boots, but they wore overalls on the line of march and in action. The cloak was white, lined with blue.

CUIRASSIERS II

1, 2. Trumpeters, 1812.
3. Corporal, 1st Regiment, marching order, 1812.
4. 9th Regiment, 1812.
5. Non-Commissioned officer, stable dress with cloak, 1812.
6. 14th Regiment, undress, 1812.

1
2
3
4
5
6

Carabiniers

In 1804, the carabiniers were still wearing the same uniform as in 1791, except for the bearskin cap which was some 20 in. in height. Their name was derived from the carbine which was their traditional weapon. They wore the French coatee, and epaulettes with scarlet fringes and white crescents. They were formed as two regiments.

In 1806, Napoleon, who held these horse grenadiers in high esteem, made his brother, Louis, Colonel-General of the 1st Regiment, and his brother-in-law, Borghese, Colonel.

In 1809, for a reason known only to himself, Napoleon converted the carabiniers into a special type of cuirassier. The simple, former uniform was replaced by a white coatee, a cuirass with front and back plates of steel covered with brass, and a 'Roman' helmet. Only two examples of this helmet, one badly damaged, still exist. It consisted of a brass body with front and back peaks and a high crest of the same metal covered with a scarlet comb. This headdress weighed some 4 lbs. 8 oz.

CARABINIERS I

1. Trumpeter, 1809–10.
2. Private, 1808.
3. Private, 1805.
4. Subaltern, 1805.

4
3
1
2

In 1809, the carabiniers were issued with the coatee using sky-blue as the distinguishing colour. The regulation of 1812 described this uniform as being without lapels, the collar and turnbacks of sky-blue with white piping on the collar and with turnback badges in the form of a white grenade. The 1st Regiment had red cuffs piped with white and cuff-slashes piped with blue, and the 2nd Regiment had sky-blue cuffs and blue cuff-slashes. Epaulettes with scarlet fringes picked out in white gave protection to the shoulders. The buckskin breeches were replaced by Hungarian breeches or by stockinette pantaloons. The traditional housings were replaced, on active service, by a sheepskin.

In addition to the carbine, the carabiniers carried two pistols and an 1800-pattern heavy cavalry sabre.

Less than three hundred of the Carabiniers returned from the disastrous Russian Campaign.

CARABINIERS II

1. Major commanding 2nd Regiment, in cloak, 1812.
2. Major, 2nd Regiment, undress, 1812.
3. Trumpeter, 1810.
4. Trumpeter, 1812.
5. 1st Regiment, 1812.
6. 2nd Regiment, 1812.
7. Service dress, 1810.
8. Colonel, 1st Regiment, 1812.

6
8
7
5
1
2
3
4

Dragoons

In Germany in 1805, the dragoons had greatly disappointed the Emperor, for they had shown that they could fight neither mounted nor on foot. Their failure was due to their officers who, in the hope of making them appear outstanding, had evolved an unnecessarily complicated drill which resulted in disorder and confusion in action. Nevertheless, at Wertingen on 8 October 1806, the dragoons redeemed their good name by taking the village house by house as a prelude to Auerstadt. Napoleon was so favourably impressed that, in the following year, he added a Regiment of Dragoons to the *Garde Impériale*.[4]

The uniform had not been changed since 1791, it was a dark green coatee with white waistcoat and breeches. The crested brass helmet had a sealskin turban and a black mane.

In 1812, the dragoons were given a coatee of the infantry pattern, but in green. The regiments were divided into five series of six each, and each series had its own distinguishing colour: 1st–6th scarlet, 7th–12th crimson, 13th–18th deep pink, 19th–24th pale yellow and 25th–30th saffron. The light troops wore busbies and epaulettes with red fringes like the pioneers.

The dragoons were armed with a straight sabre, a pistol, and a short musket of the 1777 pattern adapted to take a bayonet. By this time, the green horse furniture trimmed with white had been replaced by a white sheepskin trimmed in the colour of the regimental facing.

Having been sent to Spain where they rapidly became veteran soldiers, the dragoons acquired such a reputation that, after the disasters of 1814, their recall to France seemed the only way to save the day. At Nangis and at Provins

4. See Volume II.

DRAGOONS I (Mounted)

1. Trumpeter, 10th Regiment, 1804.
2. Dragoon, in cloak.
3. 13th Regiment, 1804–12.
4. Officer, 3rd Regiment, 1812.
5. 17th Regiment, 1812.

5
4
17
1
2
3

DRAGOONS II (Dismounted) 1804–12

1. Flank Company.
2. 23rd Regiment.
3. 28th Regiment.
4. 4th Regiment.
5. Pioneer.
6. Dragoon, in short jacket, 1806.
7. Drummer, 1805.
8. Dragoon, 1805.
9. Subaltern, 1805.

(Seine-et-Marne), the charge of the dragoons made the invaders fall back, but their heroism could not stem the tide.

For identification, the thirty regiments were divided into five series of six each. They were distinguished by the colours as listed below:

	FACINGS	CUFF-SLASHES	COLLAR	LAPELS	TURNBACKS	POCKETS
1st	Scarlet	Scarlet	Scarlet	Scarlet	Scarlet	Horizontal
2nd	Scarlet			Scarlet	Scarlet	Horizontal
3rd		Scarlet	Scarlet	Scarlet	Scarlet	Horizontal
4th		Scarlet	Scarlet	Scarlet	Scarlet	Vertical
5th	Scarlet			Scarlet	Scarlet	Vertical
6th		Scarlet	Scarlet	Scarlet	Scarlet	Vertical
7th	Crimson	Crimson	Crimson	Crimson	Crimson	Horizontal
8th	Crimson			Crimson	Crimson	Horizontal
9th		Crimson	Crimson	Crimson	Crimson	Horizontal
10th	Crimson	Crimson	Crimson	Crimson		Vertical
11th	Crimson			Crimson	Crimson	Vertical
12th		Crimson	Crimson	Crimson	Crimson	Vertical
13th	Dark Pink	Dark Pink	Dark Pink	Dark Pink	Dark Pink	Horizontal
14th	Dark Pink			Dark Pink	Dark Pink	Horizontal
15th		Dark Pink	Dark Pink	Dark Pink	Dark Pink	Horizontal
16th	Dark Pink	Dark Pink	Dark Pink	Dark Pink	Dark Pink	Vertical
17th	Dark Pink			Dark Pink	Dark Pink	Vertical
18th		Dark Pink	Dark Pink	Dark Pink	Dark Pink	Vertical
19th	Pale Yellow	Pale Yellow	Pale Yellow	Pale Yellow	Pale Yellow	Horizontal
20th	Pale Yellow			Pale Yellow	Pale Yellow	Horizontal
21st		Pale Yellow		Pale Yellow	Pale Yellow	Horizontal
22nd	Pale Yellow	Pale Yellow	Pale Yellow	Pale Yellow	Pale Yellow	Vertical
23rd	Pale Yellow			Pale Yellow	Pale Yellow	Vertical
24th		Pale Yellow	Pale Yellow	Pale Yellow	Pale Yellow	Vertical
25th	Saffron	Saffron	Saffron	Saffron	Saffron	Horizontal
26th	Saffron			Saffron	Saffron	Horizontal
27th		Saffron	Saffron	Saffron	Saffron	Horizontal
28th	Saffron	Saffron	Saffron	Saffron	Saffron	Vertical
29th	Saffron			Saffron	Saffron	Vertical
30th		Saffron	Saffron	Saffron	Saffron	Vertical

8
9
6
7
1
2
3
4
5
L. & F.
FUNCKEN

The Chasseurs à Cheval

In 1804, there were twenty-six regiments of *chasseurs à cheval*, though the 17th and 18th Regiments were notional. In this same year, seven more regiments were added to the establishment. The *chasseurs à cheval* retained the hussar uniform. Indeed, one particularly conservative regiment did so until 1813.

In 1806, the hussar jacket was replaced by a long-skirted coatee, except in the 4th, 5th, 6th, and 10th Regiments. The headdress was a black leather shako with a diamond-shaped plate and a white festoon, topped by a plume in the distinguishing colour of the regiment. The light troops wore busbies with brightly-coloured flashes and plumes.

They were armed with the 1790-pattern light cavalry sabre, a carbine 44 in. in length, and one or sometimes two pistols. The green shabracque (saddle-cloth) edged in white was replaced on service by a sheepskin.

CHASSEURS À CHEVAL I

1. 4th Regiment, 1804.
2. Flank Company, 1st Regiment, 1806.
3. 13th Regiment, 1806.
4. Trumpeter, 19th Regiment.

	COLLAR	FACINGS		COLLAR	FACINGS
1st	Scarlet	Scarlet	14th		Orange
2nd		Scarlet	15th	Orange	
3rd	Scarlet		16th	Sky Blue	Sky Blue
4th	Pale Yellow	Pale Yellow	17th	Disbanded under the Republic	
5th		Pale Yellow	18th	Disbanded under the Republic	
6th	Pale Yellow		19th	Saffron	Saffron
7th	Pink	Pink	20th		Saffron
8th		Pink	21st	Saffron	
9th	Pink		22nd	Deep Yellow	Deep Yellow
10th	Crimson	Crimson	23rd		Deep Yellow
11th		Crimson	24th	Pale Yellow	Deep Yellow
12th	Crimson		25th	Maroon	Maroon
13th	Orange	Orange	26th		Maroon

1
2
3
4

In 1808, the *chasseurs à cheval* adopted the coatee with short skirts, known as the 'Kinski' pattern.

The well-known regulations of 1812, which attempted to standardize the dress of the Imperial Army, gave the *chasseurs à cheval* a coatee with square-cut lapels, Hungarian breeches with thigh ornaments and, on service, overalls.

The light troops, too, were ordered to wear the shako, though, in fact, they carried on wearing the busby. Each regiment had its own type of shako. The 31st Regiment wore chapskas.

As light cavalry, the role of the *chasseurs à cheval* included reconnaissance and skirmishing. Nevertheless, they were equally prepared to charge a square, and they distinguished themselves in nearly every battle.

For identification, the thirty-one regiments were divided into eleven series each of three.

Their distinctive colours were as below:

CHASSEURS À CHEVAL II

1. Flank Company, 17th Regiment, 1812.
2. 16th Regiment, 1812.
3. Pioneer, 1808.
4. 1st Regiment, 1812.
5. 27th Regiment, 1812.
6. Trumpeter, 1810.

	COLLAR	COLLAR PIPING	FACINGS	PIPING		COLLAR	COLLAR PIPING	FACINGS	PIPING
1st	Scarlet	Green	Scarlet	Green	17th	Green	Sky Blue	Sky Blue	Green
2nd	Green	Scarlet	Scarlet	Green	18th	Sky Blue	Green	Green	Sky Blue
3rd	Scarlet	Green	Green	Scarlet	19th	Saffron	Green	Saffron	Green
4th	Pale Yellow	Green	Pale Yellow	Green	20th	Green	Saffron	Saffron	Green
5th	Green	Pale Yellow	Pale Yellow	Green	21st	Saffron	Green	Green	Saffron
6th	Pale Yellow	Green	Green	Pale Yellow	22nd	Deep Yellow	Green	Deep Yellow	Green
7th	Pink	Green	Pink	Green	23rd	Green	Deep Yellow	Deep Yellow	Green
8th	Green	Pink	Pink	Green	24th	Deep Yellow	Green	Green	Deep Yello
9th	Pink	Green	Green	Pink	25th	Maroon	Green	Maroon	Green
10th	Crimson	Green	Crimson	Green	26th	Green	Maroon	Maroon	Green
11th	Green	Crimson	Crimson	Green	27th	Maroon	Green	Green	Maroon
12th	Crimson	Green	Green	Crimson	28th	Purple	Green	Purple	Green
13th	Orange	Green	Orange	Green	29th	Green	Purple	Purple	Green
14th	Green	Orange	Orange	Green	30th	Purple	Green	Green	Purple
15th	Orange	Green	Green	Orange	31st	Buff	Green	Buff	Green
16th	Sky Blue	Green	Sky Blue	Green					

5
6
3
1
2
4
F.

The Chevau-légers Lanciers

The *Chevau-légers Lanciers* or Lancers were only introduced into the Imperial Army in 1811. The first brushes with the Russian Cossacks had shown the value of the lance to Napoleon, a weapon which had not been used by the French. As a result, three regiments of lancers were raised in Poland[5] and, soon afterwards, six regiments of *chevau-légers lanciers* were added to the establishment. The men were drawn from the dragoons.

The lance carried by these regiments was 9 ft. long. This, as well as a light cavalry sabre, a pistol and a carbine, made a heavy and cumbersome load for the horsemen, and it was not unusual for them to throw away either the lance or the carbine at the first opportunity.

The uniform was a dark green coatee, with figured pockets. The collar, lapels, cuffs, and turnbacks were in the distinguishing colour: scarlet for the 1st Regiment, saffron yellow for the 2nd, pink for the 3rd, crimson for the 4th, sky-blue for the 5th, and maroon for the 6th Regiment.

5. See Volume II.

CHEVAU-LÉGERS LANCIERS I

1. 5th Regiment.
2. Trumpeter, 3rd Regiment, 1812.

2
1

The collar was piped in green, and the epaulettes and pocket-flaps were piped in the distinguishing colour. The turnback badges were in the form of a green eagle. The light troops had red epaulettes. The Hungarian-style breeches were green, and had thigh-ornaments. On service, the lancers wore green strapped and booted overalls, with coloured stripes. The helmet was of the dragoon pattern with a black crest, except for the trumpeters whose crest was white. The light cavalrys' boots were trimmed with yellow.

The horse furniture consisted of a sheepskin, with a saw-toothed edge of cloth in the distinguishing colour of the regiment.

As in most other arms of the service, the officers wore the same dress as the men, but made of finer cloth and laced with gold. The epaulettes, belts, boots, and shabracque were similarly laced.

Introduced when times were bad, the elegant lancers made their name during the Russian campaign, ending up at Waterloo where, in company with the cuirassiers, they made repeated desperate charges to the cry of *Vive l'Empereur*!

CHEVAU-LÉGERS LANCIERS II

1. 5th Regiment.
2. 6th Regiment.
3. Major Commanding, 1812.
4. Trumpeter, 5th Regiment, 1811.
5. Trumpeter, 3rd Regiment, 1812.

1
2
3
5

The Gendarmerie[6]

It was in Spain, between 1808 and 1814, that the gendarmerie proved themselves as fighting troops. The *petite gendarmerie d'Espagne* frequently displayed great courage in battle. The corps returned to France in 1814 to help stem the Allied invasion, and, like the dragoons, distinguished themselves at Nangis and at Montereau.

The gendarmes wore cocked hats trimmed with silver. Their coatees were blue with collar, lapels, turnbacks and cuff-slashes in red and red epaulettes trimmed with white. The waistcoat and breeches were of buff leather. The mounted men wore dragoon pattern boots, and the dismounted men black gaiters.

They were armed with a light cavalry sabre and a carbine. The horse furniture was similar to that of the cuirassiers.

Marshal Suchet dismounted one squadron of lancers-gendarmes to deal more efficiently with the bands of guerillas. This unit wore a blue coatee with blue lapels, scarlet collar, cuffs, and turnbacks, and a white aiguillette on the left shoulder. The hussar-style waistcoat was red, and the Hungarian-style breeches were blue with white thigh-ornaments. The shako was trimmed with white and had a red plume.

The *gendarmerie métropolitaine* (that is, the gendarmerie in France) wore blue coatees with red collars and lapels, blue cuffs and cuff-slashes piped in red, and red turnbacks with blue grenade skirt-ornaments. On the left shoulder, they wore a white aiguillette.

Among their duties, the *gendarmerie métropolitaine* had the thankless task of picking up deserters and men avoiding military service, whose numbers grew yearly and who tried to hide in the remoter parts of the countryside.

6. The Gendarmerie of the *Garde Impériale* is included in Volume II.

GENDARMERIE

1. Gendarme, dismounted branch, 1810.
2. Gendarme, mounted branch, for service with the Line, 1810.
3. Gendarme, serving in Spain, 1810.
4. Lancier-gendarme, serving in Spain, 1813.

3
4
2
1
R.F. FUNCKEN

The Hussars

From thirteen regiments in 1793, the number of hussar regiments was reduced to twelve in 1799 and ten in 1803.

With their pelisses, dolmans and sabretaches, the hussars were the most colourful mounted troops of the Empire and the regiments vied with each other in their attempts to appear the most elegant. Dressed so obviously, they had to be brave, and they often made raids deep into the enemy lines without worrying whether they might be cut off themselves.

In 1804, the hussars wore black shakos with white festoons and plumes in the distinguishing colour. They wore their hair in plaits at the sides and back, as a protection against sword-cuts. They were armed with the 1792-pattern sabres and the 1786-pattern carbines.

The ten regiments were distinguished, in 1804, as follows:

HUSSARS I

1–12. Forage caps, 1st to 12th Regiments.
13. Pouch and pouch belt.
14. Hussar saddle, covered with sheepskin, with valise, 10th Regiment, 1812.
15. Carbine belt.
16. 8th Regiment, 1804–6.
17. 1st Regiment, 1807.
18. 11th Regiment, full dress, 1810.
19. 8th Regiment, winter service dress, 1809.

	PELISSE	DOLMAN	WAISTCOAT	BREECHES	CUFFS	BUTTONS
1st	Sky Blue	Sky Blue	Scarlet	Sky Blue	Scarlet	White
2nd	Chestnut	Chestnut	Sky Blue	Sky Blue	Sky Blue	White
3rd	Silver Grey	Silver Grey	Silver Grey	Silver Grey	Scarlet	White
4th	Scarlet	Royal Blue	White	Royal Blue	Scarlet	Brass
5th	White	Sky Blue	Sky Blue	Sky Blue	White	Brass
6th	Royal Blue	Scarlet	Scarlet	Royal Blue	Scarlet	Brass
7th	Dark Green, fur-trimmed	Dark Green & scarlet collar	Scarlet	Scarlet	Scarlet	Brass
8th	Dark Green	Dark Green & scarlet collar	Scarlet	Scarlet	Scarlet	White
9th	Scarlet	Scarlet & sky-blue collar	Scarlet	Scarlet	Scarlet	Brass
10th	Sky Blue	Sky Blue & scarlet collar	Scarlet	Sky Blue	Scarlet	White

2
3
4
5
6
7
8
9
10
11
12
16
17
18
19
13
14
15
F. FUNCKEN.

HUSSARS II

1. Trumpeter, 1st Regiment, 1807.
2. Trumpeter, 7th Regiment, 1807.
3. 10th Regiment, 1806.
4. 1st Regiment, 1808.
5. 4th Regiment, 1815.
6. 12th Regiment, 1813.
7. 11th Regiment, 1810.
8. 2nd Regiment, 1812.
9. 6th Regiment, 1807.
10. 3rd Regiment, 1810.
11. Flank Squadron, 7th Regiment, 1808.
12. 5th Regiment, 1808.
13. 8th Regiment, 1809.
14. 9th Regiment, 1810.

10
11
12
13
14
9
7
5
6

In 1810, a new 11th Regiment was raised from the Dutch Hussars, and this was the only regiment that had the pelisse trimmed with white sheepskin. Their light troop wore white bear-skin busbies. In the same year, a new 12th regiment was raised from a squadron of the 9th Hussars in Spain. They wore the same uniform as the 9th Hussars, and was numbered 2nd/9th Hussars.

In 1812, the regiments used the following distinguishing colours:

	PELISSE	BRAID AND LACE	DOLMAN	COLLAR	FACINGS
1st	Sky Blue	White	Sky Blue	Sky Blue	Red
2nd	Chestnut	White	Chestnut	Chestnut	Sky Blue
3rd	Silver Grey	Red	Silver Grey	Silver Grey	Red
4th	Scarlet	Yellow	Imperial Blue	Imperial Blue	Scarlet
5th	White	Lemon	Sky Blue	Sky Blue	White
6th	Imperial Blue	Yellow	Scarlet	Scarlet	Scarlet
7th	Dark Green	Yellow	Dark Green	Scarlet	Scarlet
8th	Dark Green	White	Dark Green	Scarlet	Scarlet
9th	Sky Blue	Yellow	Scarlet	Sky Blue	Sky Blue
10th	Sky Blue	White	Sky Blue	Scarlet	Scarlet
11th	Imperial blue	Yellow	Imperial blue	Scarlet	Scarlet

	BREECHES	WAISTCOAT	BUTTONS	SASH
1st	Green	Scarlet	White	Crimson and White
2nd	Sky Blue	Sky Blue	White	Crimson and White
3rd	Silver Grey	Silver Grey	White	Crimson and White
4th	Imperial Blue	Imperial Blue	Brass	Crimson and Yellow
5th	Sky Blue	Sky Blue	Brass	Crimson and Yellow
6th	Imperial Blue	Scarlet	White	Crimson and Yellow
7th	Scarlet	Scarlet	Brass	Crimson and Yellow
8th	Scarlet	Scarlet	Brass	Crimson and White
9th	Light Blue	Light Blue	Brass	Crimson and Yellow
10th	Sky Blue	Scarlet	White	Crimson and White
11th	Imperial Blue	Scarlet	Brass	Crimson and Yellow

The hussars soon gained their laurels. In the 10th Regiment, which had been awarded 25 crosses of the *Legion d'Honneur*[7] by the Emperor on the eve of the Battle of Lützen, 2 May 1813, only five of those decorated answered the roll call on the following evening.

7. This was the only French gallantry award of that time; it had been instituted by Napoleon at Boulogne in May 1802.

HUSSARS III

1. 8th Regiment, 1812.
2. 1st Regiment, 1815.
3. 8th Regiment, 1812.
4. Cornet, 8th Regiment, 1814.
5. Trumpeter, 8th Regiment, 1812.
6. Trumpeter, 1st Regiment, 1815..

4
5
6
3
1
2

The Artillery

The artillery of the Napoleonic era consisted of 4 pounders, 8 pounders, and 12 pounders and of 6 in. howitzers. With some modifications, this was what had been introduced by Gribeauval in 1766.

The cast-iron cannon balls were as dangerous from ricochets as from direct hits. The optimum range was between 500 and 1,000 yards according to the calibre, but the 4 pounders could be effective up to 1,300 yards and the 12 pounder up to 1,800 yards. When the enemy were sufficiently close, grape-shot and shrapnel were used. The latter consisted of a cannister that discharged shot in much the same way as the cartridge in a shot-gun. The ball was attached to a 'sabot' i.e. a wooden disc which served to keep it evenly in place in the bore and which fitted into the mouth of the charge-bag.

The gun was loaded by inserting this elementary cartridge into the muzzle and ramming it together with a straw wad. The charge-bag was then pierced with the vent-bit which was inserted through the touch-hole. Finally, the priming-charge was poured into the vent, when lit the gun fired.

FOOT ARTILLERY

1. Gunner, 1812.
2. Gunner, undress, 1809.
3. Subaltern, 1812.
4. Gunner, 1812.
5. Drummer, 1812.
6. Drummer, 1810.
7. Gunner, 1806.
8. Lieutenant, 1811.
9. Colonel, 1806.
10. Gunner, 1806.

8
9
10
1
2
3
4
5
6

The ammunition was transported in waggons, each carrying forty-eight to a hundred solid-shot and twenty to fifty cannister-shot. According to the calibre, each gun had from two to five waggons allotted. In addition, each gun had a small ammunition limber carrying nine to eighteen solid shot which could be used in an emergency, while waiting for the waggons to come up.

The howitzer fired hollow spherical shells filled with powder and fused. According to the length of the fuse, these could be timed to explode in the air or on the ground. These shells were particularly effective as incendiaries and for the destruction of hastily fortified houses. All the artillery could keep up a rate of fire of between one and two rounds a minute. In addition to this field artillery, there was also the fortress artillery and the coast artillery, which consisted mostly of 10-in. and 12-in. pieces.

The field artillery was drawn by horses ridden by men of the artillery train, each piece having a team of four horses.

HORSE ARTILLERY AND ARTILLERY TRAIN

1. Officer, Horse Artillery, 1806.
2. Ammunition waggon, Artillery Train, 1804–6.
3. Gun and limber, drawn by Artillery Train, 1813.
4. Trumpeter, Horse Artillery, 1806.
5. Gunner, Horse Artillery, 1806.

1
2
5
3
4

The number of men required to serve a gun varied with the calibre from eight to fifteen. By the nature of its work, the artillery train tended to support the fighting troops, rather than itself to take part in the battle. The stoicism of these men and their disregard for danger earned them a reputation for bravery that was not undeserved.

In 1806, their uniform was an iron-grey coatee with lapels, collar and cuffs of dark blue. The shako was black with a white-metal plate in the form of a lozenge.

At the fall of the Empire, there were twenty-six battalions. Napoleon, who never had enough guns, increased the strength of the artillery to compensate what he considered to be a deterioration in the infantry. This had been brought about by the steady disappearance of experienced men, as a result of the successive campaigns.

Exclusive of the artillery of the *Garde Impériale*,[8] in the last days of the Empire there were three hundred companies of artillery, each of six or eight pieces. These were formed into

8. The artillery of the *Garde Impériale* is dealt with in Volume II.

HORSE ARTILLERY

1. Gunner, 1805.
2, 3. Gunners, 1812.
4. Gunner, 1810.

3
4
1
2

nine regiments of foot artillery and six regiments of horse artillery. The men were highly disciplined and brave, and were prepared to die fighting their guns.

Their uniform was a blue coatee with the collar, cuffs and lapels in blue piped with red. The turnbacks were red, the waistcoat and breeches were blue, and the leggings were black. The black shako had the pompom, lacing and festoons in red. The foot artillery were armed with a short musket and bayonet, which could be slung when the guns were in action, they also carried a short sword for self-defence.

The horse artillery were armed like the light cavalry. Up to 1812, the uniform was of the hussar-style, blue with red facings and lace. Later, they wore blue coatees with scarlet cuffs and turnbacks, and blue collars and lapels. The shako had a scarlet pompom and riding boots were worn.

With the exception of the ironwork which was black, the guns were painted a yellowish olive, termed *gros vert*. This was made by mixing thirty parts of black with 2,500 parts of yellow ochre.

ARTILLERY AND ARTILLERY TRAIN

1. Gunner, Horse Artillery, 1804.
2. Gunner, Horse Artillery, wearing cloak, 1812.
3. 6-in Howitzer.
4. Lieutenant, Foot Artillery, 1811.
5. Non-Commissioned officer, Horse Artillery, 1806.
6. Artillery Train, 1813.
7. 4 pounder gun.
8. Artillery Train, 1813.
9. Driver, Artillery Train, 1806.
10. Trumpeter, Artillery Train, 1812.
11. Trumpeter, Horse Artillery, 1812.

12, 13. Gunners, Coast Artillery, 1809 and 1812.

1
2
3
4
5
6
7
8
10
11
12
13
L.F

The Medical Services

Of all the services in Napoleon's armies, the medical service was the worst-organised. It was only the selfless devotion of the medical officers that alleviated the miseries of the wounded and the sick in any way.

The celebrated army surgeon, Baron Larrey (1766–1842), who introduced the ambulance, i.e. a vehicle for carrying stretcher-cases, in 1797, fought continually against the indifference that made the wounded grenadier say 'We all know that nobody cares if we're wounded, so why don't they kill us and be done with it!'

Most of the army surgeons were incompetent, and many of them were young men of good family who chose the medical profession as a means of avoiding being called-up in a combatant branch.

In the opinion of a Larrey or a Percy,[9] both dedicated members of their profession, there was an equal duty to help friend and foe. However, this was far from universal and it was not until after the 1st Geneva Convention had been agreed under the auspices of the Red Cross in 1864 that medical treatment was extended to the captured enemy as a matter of course.

9. Pierre-Francois Percy (1754–1825), an army surgeon, who invented the *Würst*, a small vehicle for carrying the medical orderlies, and also the stretcher.

MEDICAL SERVICES

1. Medical Orderly, service dress, 1812.
2. Surgeon, marching order, 1814.
3. Medical Orderly, 1812.
4. Surgeon's Mate.
5. Medical Orderly, with collapsible stretcher.
6. Ambulance, as designed by Larrey, 1805.

1
2
3
4
5
6

The Engineers and Bridgers

The bridging companies will always be associated in French military history with the crossing of the Berezina in November 1812, which was only one of many occasions when these troops played a vital rôle in the outcome of the battle.

They wore the uniform of the artillery to which they were attached. Also seconded from the artillery, the miners were transferred to the engineers in 1793 at the instance of Carnot,[10] creator of the fourteen Armies of the Republic. By an imperial decree, the companies of miners were increased in number to sixteen and were organised in two battalions. Although few in number, the miners were highly skilled, and the war in Spain afforded them many opportunities of proving their worth, notably so at the siege of Saragossa in 1808–9.

The sappers wore the same uniform as the miners, but were a separate corps and which consisted in 1813 of five battalions. Their uniform was a blue coatee with the collar, lapels, cuffs and cuff-slashes in black velvet piped in red. They wore the infantry shako; however, on active service the sappers wore black helmets and breast-plates. In 1810, an engineer company in the *Garde Impériale* was raised.[11]

10. General Lazare Nicolas Marguerite Carnot (1753–1823) was a prominent figure in the French Revolution and was also the author of a book on fortifications. See *Arms and Uniforms II – 18th Century to the Present Day*.

11. See Volume II.

ENGINEERS, ENGINEER TRAIN AND MISCELLANEOUS SERVICES

1. Sapper, 1809.
2. Engineer Officer, 1805.
3. Sapper, 1808.
4. Driver, Supply Train.
5. Engineer Train, 1806.
6. Marine, 1810.
7. Veteran, 1806.
8. Dockyard Battalion, 1812.
9. Local Defence Unit, 1812.
10. Customs, 1814.

1
2
3
4
5
6
7
8
9
10

The engineer train was raised in 1806 and the supply train was set up in 1807, replacing the civilian contractors who frequently starved the army of necessary supplies.

In addition to these corps, there were others, even less well-known, like the veterinary service who wore blue piped with white, buckskin breeches and hussar boots. There were also the labour corps and the frontier guards; the latter were organised by the generals commanding the military districts that lay along the frontiers of France. Other little known services were the gunpowder factories and the postal service with its imperial green uniform. Finally, there were the marines and the dockyard workers who were absorbed into the infantry of the line in 1812. Old soldiers, no longer fit for general service were drafted into the veteran companies. No longer of any use, they had become a burden on the State, and these men, who had contributed so much to the glorification of the Empire, now saw the administration reduce their meagre pension day by day.

ARMS

1. Musket, pattern 1786.
2. Musket, pattern 1801.
3. Cavalry pistol, pattern 1801.
4. Cavalry pistol, pattern 1805.
5. Cavalry pistol, pattern 1777.
6. Fusil, pattern 1777 modified in 1801.
7. Short sword, pattern 1803.
8. Light Cavalry sword.
9. Chasseur's sword.
10. Light Cavalry sword, pattern 1803.
11. Sword, pattern 1796.
12. Sword, pattern 1803.

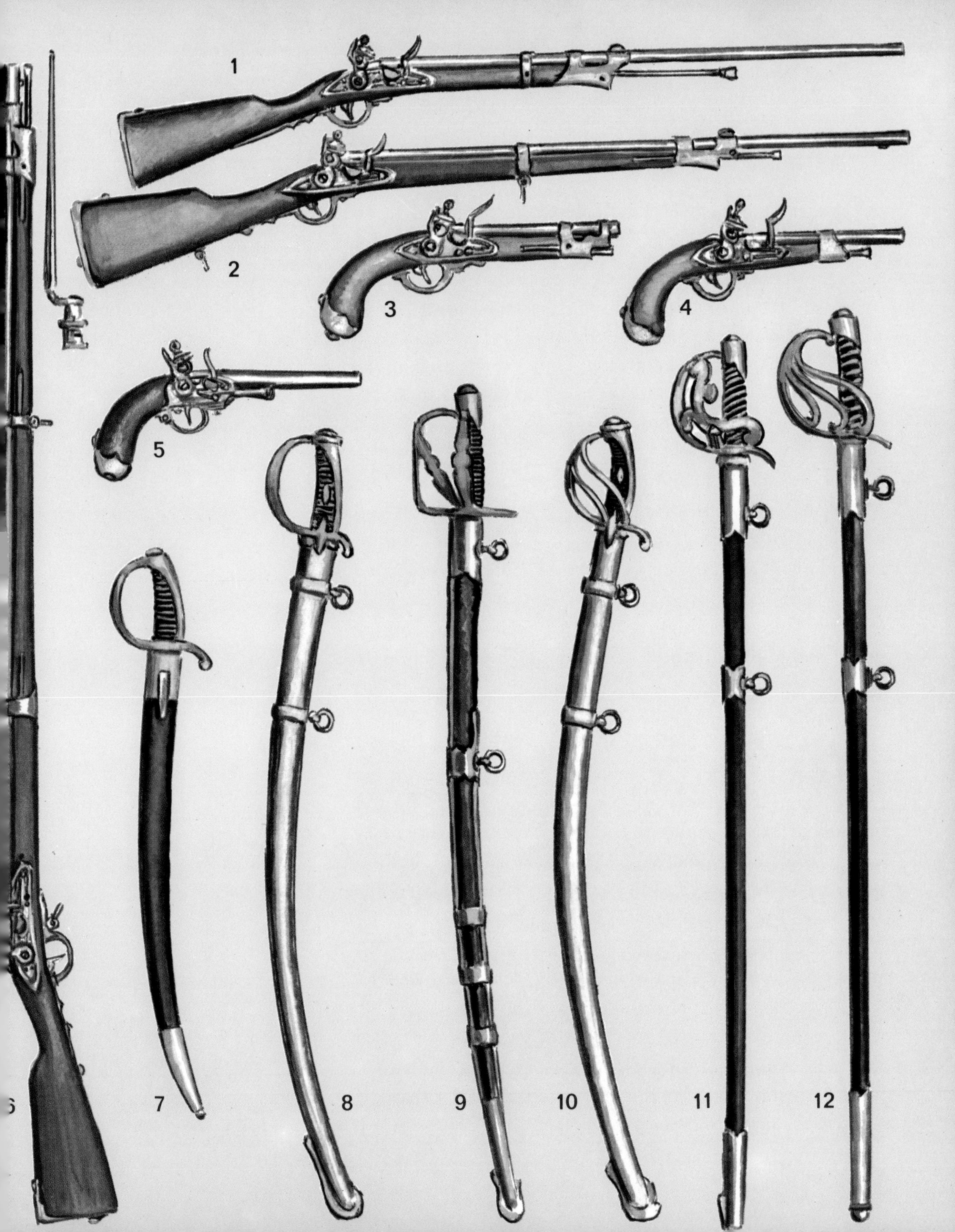
1
2
3
4
5
6
7
8
9
10
11
12

The Military Schools

Before the Revolution, there were thirteen military schools scattered throughout the kingdom and only youths of good family were eligible for admission. Under the Republic, the doors were thrown open to every citizen, which resulted in such anarchy that the Convention closed all of them except the school at Auxerre.

In 1794, the Convention established the *École de Mars*, whose students wore a uniform conceived by David, and lived a spartan life in tents; this only lasted four months. Six months later, the School of Public Works was opened and, on 1 September 1795, this became the *École Polytechnique*. Under the Empire, there was a Governor and the pupils had to provide their own clothing, pay an annual fee of 800 francs and buy their books and other requirements themselves.

In 1802, the *École Spéciale Militaire* was opened at Fontainebleau, and this was moved to Saint-Cyr under the Empire. The students were formed in two battalions and underwent intensive military training, including geography, history, drawing, geometry, survey, public speaking, equitation and swimming. Another military school run on the same lines, the *Prytanée*, was set up at La Flèche.

In 1809, Napoleon conceived the idea of the *École Spéciale de Cavalerie*, which was intended to attract the well-to-do young with a taste for riding to the Army. In due course, the students were posted to the cavalry with the rank of second lieutenant. The school was opened in the Château of Saint-Germain, but, after the restoration of the Bourbons, it moved to Saumur four years later.

MILITARY SCHOOLS

1–3. St Germain, 1809, 1811, and Flank Company, 1811.
4. La Flèche, 1814.
5, 6. St Cyr, 1809, 1813.
7. Polytechnique, 1809.
8. Fontainebleau, 1804.

1 2 3 4

5 6 7 8

Eagles and Standards

On 5 December 1804, Napoleon presented new standards to the Army. The finial of the staff was in the form of an eagle with its wings half-spread, which led to the standards being commonly known as Eagles, the more so as often only the staff, without the flag, was carried in action.

By an order of 18 February 1808, a *porte-aigle* or standard bearer, was added to the establishment of the light infantry and the line regiments. The Eagles were carried by ensigns (second lieutenants) of not less than ten years' service who had fought at Ulm, Austerlitz, Jena, and Friedland. The officer carrying the Eagle was styled the 'first eagle-bearer', and he was accompanied by two old soldiers styled the 'second eagle-bearer' and the 'third eagle-bearer', all three of whom were nominated personally by the Emperor. The second and third eagle-bearers carried spontoons, that of the second bearing a red pennant and that of the third a white one. Both were also armed with two pistols carried in a breast-holster.

The escort to the standard was generally drawn from the centre companies, since the flank companies were liable to be detached from the main body, which conformed with the Emperor's wishes in this matter.

COLOUR PARTIES

1, 3. Non-Commissioned officers of Colour Party.
2. Ensign.

An Imperial Order of 1808 directed that Colour Parties would wear bearskins without badges. The colour shown is the pattern used during the Hundred Days.

1
2
3
F. FUNCKEN

Mounted Bands

In 1802, Napoleon, then First Consul, abolished mounted bands and raised four new and badly-needed cavalry regiments from the horses then made available.

When circumstances improved, the mounted bands were brought back, and normally consisted of sixteen trumpets, six horns, and three trombones. The hussars and the carabiniers had kettle-drums, but the other classes of cavalry had bands organised on the same lines as the infantry who played only upon ceremonial occasions.[12]

Sometimes the musicians wore a coatee in the reversed colours of the regiment, but often their dress was quite different. Their headdresses were often bizarre in the extreme, and trumpeters in the cuirassiers wore busbies or white bearskins, or replaced the regulation white crest with the bearskin crest of the carabiniers.

The kettle-drummers went to even further extremes, achieving what can only be compared to circus uniforms.

Among the more unusual instruments played by military musicians were the bassoon and the serpent. The bassoon, still very primitive at the beginning of the eighteenth

12. The mounted bands of the *Garde Impériale* will be dealt with in Volume II.

MOUNTED BANDS

1. Bassoon-player, Dragoons, 1808.
2. Cornet-player, Hussars, 1810.
3, 4. Trombone-players, *Chasseurs à Cheval*, 1806.

2
3
4
1

century, was modified in about 1750 by the addition of two more keys which brought the total to four, and a fifth was introduced about 1760. Since then, numerous improvements to the instruments have been made. Even stranger was the serpent of which the long thick tube was bent into the form of an 'S', so that it resembled in shape the animal of which it bore the name.

The serpent dated from the middle of the fifteenth century, when it was used to accompany church choirs. The instrument was used in its original form in the French Army, but an improved type was developed in England in about 1800. This was made of copper or brass and was in the shape of a trombone with the mouth in the shape of a dragon's head. This was called a bass-horn. It was introduced into France by the Allies in 1815, and was known variously as an English serpent or a Russian bassoon.

The art of playing the French serpent was the subject of a work, *Méthode du Serpent* which was published in 1799 by François-Joseph Gossec (1733–1829), one of the founders of the Paris Conservatory.

KETTLE DRUMMERS

1. Dragoons, 1807.
2. Hussars, 1810.
3. Carabiniers.
4. *Chasseurs à Cheval.*

4
3
2
1

THE BRITISH ARMY

General Officers & the Infantry

The British were the most persistent opponents of Napoleon. Initially, the revolutionary reforms were received in England with some optimism and a smiling condescension at the eccentricities of the French. Subsequent events and, in particular, the advent of the 'Corsican adventurer' and his policy of conquest soon changed their attitude, and Britain found herself involved in one of the greatest struggles of her history.

Napoleon's projected invasion of England and the assembling of his Army of Invasion on the coast near Boulogne, caused considerable anxiety. However, the British accepted the challenge and set about preparing a warm welcome for the enemy. The victory of Trafalgar destroyed any hopes of a landing and the country was given a breathing-space; but having realised the true extent of the threat, she prepared herself for a prolonged struggle.

Until 1800, the British Army as a whole had worn hats, apart from the Light Dragoons, the Horse Artillery and the Grenadiers. At that time, the infantry adopted a black leather shako of the Austrian pattern, known as the 'stove-pipe' shako. This was adorned with a plume, white for the grenadier companies, green for the light infantry companies, and red and white for the battalion companies.

The General Officers, who were part of the Army Staff, wore close-fitting scarlet uniforms with a narrow turnback to the skirts. They were lapelled to the waist, and could be cross-buttoned. A crimson sash was worn round the waist, tied on the left in the infantry, and on the right by other officers. The collar, lapels, cuffs, and button-holes were embroidered in gold. The epaulettes were also decorated in

BRITISH OFFICERS I

1. Lieutenant-General, 1808.
2. Major-General, 1810.
3. Company Officer, Light Infantry Company, 1812.
4. Lieutenant-General, 1813.
5. Sergeant, Grenadier Company, 1807.
6. Officer, 95th Rifles, 1807.
7. Field Officer, Infantry of the Line, 1807.

7
5
1
2
3
4

gold as were the tassels on the hat and on the short boots of the light cavalry. There were many divergences from the regulations, although probably fewer than in the French Army.

The regulations were adhered to more strictly in the case of the other ranks. Generally the infantry wore red, their headdress was a black 'stove-pipe' shako with a large brass plate bearing the regimental number and the badge. The coatee had short tails, and was without lapels, while the open-necked collar, the cuffs, and the turnbacks were in the distinctive colour of the regiment. Regiments were also distinguished by the spacing of the buttons and the shape of the loops round the button-holes. The grenadier companies wore bearskins, and the light infantry companies were distinguished by green shako plumes and a bugle horn on each epaulette. The practice of powdering the hair was discontinued in 1808, to the relief of all ranks.

In 1809 during the Peninsular War, the 'stove-pipe' shako was replaced by a new type known as the Wellington shako. This was made of black felt and had a frontal that rose about an inch above the crown. The plate was oval, baroque in style and smaller than its predecessor; it usually bore the Royal Cypher and the regimental number. The front of the shako was ornamented with a festoon and there was a worsted or feather plume fixed into a black cockade. This shako was lighter than the 'stove-pipe' and more becoming, furthermore, it was unlike any other shako in use at that time.

The unit was the battalion which was divided into ten companies, that on the right flank was composed of grenadiers and that on the left was composed of light infantry.

BRITISH OFFICERS II

1, 4. Major-Generals, 1815.
2, 3. Lieutenant-Generals, 1815.
5. The Duke of Wellington.
6. Cavalry Staff Corps, 1815.

6
5
1
2
3
4

Normally a battalion was five-hundred strong. In the face of the enemy, they were drawn up in two ranks with the front kneeling, a formation that could produce deadly fire. The British musket, the famous Brown Bess, fired a ball one third heavier than that of the French and of a larger calibre (0.75 in.).

To resist cavalry charges, the British infantry formed squares, each side four ranks deep. The front rank took up the kneeling position with the butt of the musket on the ground, inclined forward, with the bayonet fixed.[13] The second rank stood, with the musket and bayonet at the high port. The third and fourth ranks kept up a steady fire which was most effective, despite the fact that it took twenty motions to reload. It was due in large measure to the Duke of Wellington (1769–1852) that the infantry achieved so high a standard of efficiency.

The Iron Duke, having received his education at Eton and at the Military Academy of Angers in France, had seen service in Flanders in 1794 and 1795. On his return from India in 1805, the young Major-General had to wait until the beginning of the Peninsular War in 1807 before he had a chance to show his prowess and to put into practice on the battlefields of Europe the theories of warfare that he had developed in India. However, it was not until the final battle of the struggle at Waterloo that the two great enemies faced each other on a battlefield.

At the end of the Napoleonic wars, the British Infantry was composed of the following regiments:

13. As the pike men of the previous century carried their pikes. See *Arms and Uniforms I – Ancient Egypt to the 18th Century*.

INFANTRY OF THE LINE I

1. Light Infantry Company, 5th Foot, 1815.
2. 32nd Foot, 1814–15.
3. Private, winter dress, 1812–15.
4. Officer, winter dress, 1812–15.
5. Pioneer, 66th Foot, 1813.
6. 23rd Foot, 1815.
7. 69th Foot, 1812.
8. Light Infantry Company, 64th Foot, 1815.

1
2
3
4
5
6
7
8

GUARD REGIMENTS	FACINGS	LACE (O.R.'s White)
1st Foot Guards (Grenadier)	Blue	Gold
2nd Foot Guards (Coldstream)	Blue	Gold
3rd Foot Guards (Scots)	Blue	Gold

LINE REGIMENTS		
1st Regiment, The Royal Scots	Blue	Gold
2nd or The Queen's Royal Regiment	Blue	Silver
3rd Regiment, The Buffs (East Kent)	Buff	Silver
4th or The King's Own, Regiment	Blue	Gold
5th or The Northumberland Regiment of Foot	Green	Silver
6th or The 1st Warwickshire Regiment	Yellow	Silver
7th Regiment, The Royal Fusiliers	Blue	Gold
8th or The King's Regiment	Blue	Gold
9th or The East Norfolk Regiment	Yellow	Silver
10th or The North Lincolnshire Regiment	Yellow	Silver
11th or The North Devonshire Regiment	Dark Green	Gold
12th or The East Suffolk Regiment	Yellow	Gold
13th or The 1st Somersetshire Regiment	Yellow	Silver
14th or The Buckinghamshire Regiment	Buff	Silver
15th or The Yorkshire (East Riding) Regiment	Yellow	Silver
16th or The Bedfordshire Regiment	Yellow	Silver
17th or The Leicestershire Regiment	White	Silver
18th or The Royal Irish Regiment	Blue	Gold
19th or The 1st Yorkshire (North Riding) Regiment	Green	Gold
20th or The East Devonshire Regiment	Yellow	Silver
21st or The Royal North British Fusiliers	Blue	Gold
22nd or The Cheshire Regiment	Buff	Gold
23rd Regiment or The Royal Welsh Fusiliers	Blue	Gold
24th or The Warwickshire Regiment	Green	Silver
25th Regiment or The King's Own Borderers	Blue	Gold
26th or The Cameronian Regiment	Yellow	Silver
27th or The Inniskilling Regiment	Buff	Gold
28th or The North Gloucestershire Regiment	Yellow	Silver
29th or The Worcestershire Regiment	Yellow	Silver
30th or The Cambridgeshire Regiment	Pale Yellow	Silver
31st or The Huntingdonshire Regiment	Buff	Silver
32nd or The Cornwall Regiment	White	Gold
33rd or The 1st Yorkshire (West Riding) Regiment	Red	Silver
34th or The Cumberland Regiment	Yellow	Silver
35th or The Sussex Regiment	Orange	Silver
36th or The Herefordshire Regiment	Green	Gold
37th or The North Hampshire Regiment	Yellow	Silver
38th or The 1st Staffordshire Regiment	Yellow	Silver

LIGHT INFANTRY AND RIFLES

1. 5th Battalion, 60th Foot, with Baker carbine, 1812.
2. 95th Rifles, 1807.
3. Officer, 52nd Foot, 1812.
4, 5. Privates, 52nd Foot, 1815.

3
4
5
1
2

	FACINGS	LACE (O.R.'s White)
39th or The Dorsetshire Regiment	Pea Green	Gold
40th or The 2nd Somersetshire Regiment	Buff	Gold
41st Regiment	Red	Silver
42nd or The Royal Highland Regiment	Blue	Gold
44th or The East Essex Regiment	Yellow	Silver
45th or The Nottinghamshire Regiment	Dark Green	Silver
46th or The South Devonshire Regiment	Pale Yellow	Silver
47th or The Lancashire Regiment	White	Silver
48th or The Northamptonshire Regiment	Buff	Gold
49th or The Hertfordshire Regiment	Green	Gold
50th or The West Kent Regiment	Black	Silver
53rd or The West Shropshire Regiment	Red	Gold
54th or The West Norfolk Regiment	Green	Silver
55th or The Westmorland Regiment	Green	Gold
56th or The West Essex Regiment	Purple	Silver
57th or The West Middlesex Regiment	Yellow	Gold
58th or The Rutlandshire Regiment	Black	Gold
59th or The 2nd Nottinghamshire Regiment	White	Gold
61st or The South Gloucestershire Regiment	Buff	Silver
62nd or The Wiltshire Regiment	Buff	Silver
63rd or The West Suffolk Regiment	Dark Green	Silver
64th or The 2nd Staffordshire Regiment	Black	Gold
65th or The 2nd Yorkshire (North Riding) Regiment	White	Gold
66th or The Berkshire Regiment	Green	Gold
67th or The South Hampshire Regiment	Yellow	Silver
69th or The South Lincolnshire Regiment	Green	Gold
70th or The Glasgow Lowland Regiment	Black	Gold
72nd Highland Regiment	Yellow	Silver
73rd Highland Regiment	Dark Green	Gold
74th Highland Regiment	White	Gold
75th Highland Regiment	Yellow	Silver
76th Regiment	Red	Silver
77th or The East Middlesex Regiment	Yellow	Silver
78th Highland Regiment, The Ross-shire Buffs	Buff	Gold
79th Regiment of Cameronian Highlanders	Dark Green	Gold
80th Regiment or The Staffordshire Volunteers	Yellow	Gold
81st Regiment	Buff	Silver
82nd Regiment or The Prince of Wales' Volunteers	Yellow	Silver
83rd Regiment	Yellow	Gold
84th or The York and Lancaster Regiment	Yellow	Silver
86th or The Royal County Down Regiment	Blue	Silver
87th or The Prince of Wales' Own Irish Regiment	Green	Gold

FOOT GUARDS

1–3. Privates, Grenadier Company, 1st Foot Guards (Grenadiers), Coldstream Guards, and 3rd Foot Guards (Scots), 1812–15.

4, 6, 7. Privates, 1st Foot Guards, Coldstream Guards, and 3rd Foot Guards, 1806.

5. Private, Light Infantry Company, 3rd Foot Guards.

4
5
6
7
1
2
3

	FACINGS	LACE (O.R.'s White)
88th Regiment, The Connaught Rangers	Yellow	Silver
89th Regiment	Black	Gold
90th Regiment or The Perthshire Volunteers	Buff	Gold
91st Regiment	Yellow	Silver
92nd Regiment	Yellow	Silver
93rd Regiment	Yellow	Silver
94th Regiment	Green	Gold
96th Regiment	Buff	Silver
97th or The Queen's Own Regiment	Blue	Silver
98th Regiment	Buff	Silver
99th or The Prince of Wales' Tipperary Regiment	Pale Yellow	
100th or His Royal Highness the Prince Regent's County of Dublin Regiment	Dark Yellow	
101st or The Duke of York's Irish Regiment	White	
102nd Regiment	Yellow	Silver
103rd Regiment	White	
104th Regiment	Buff	

Lieutenant-General Sir John Moore (1761–1809) conceived the idea of introducing into the British Army Light Infantry who would match the French Voltigeurs. Initially, he converted his own Regiment, the 43rd, and this was followed by five others:

43rd or The Monmouthshire Regiment	White	Silver
51st or The 2nd Yorkshire (West Riding) Regiment	Green	Gold
52nd or The Oxfordshire Regiment	Buff	Silver
68th or The Durham Regiment	Dark Green	Silver
71st Highland Regiment	Buff	Silver
85th Regiment or The Bucks Volunteers	Yellow	Silver

Finally, as a result of experience gained in the War of American Independence, a 'super-light' class of infantry was formed, based on the German Jägers. They wore dark green, a colour known as rifle green, and were armed with the Baker carbine and a sword-bayonet. There were two battalions, the 5th Battalion, 60th Foot with scarlet facings and the 95th Regiment with black facings.

The Scottish Highland Regiments were distinguished by their feather bonnets and their tartan kilts. Lowland Regiments were dressed like the rest of the Infantry of the Line. The Duke of Wellington received his first commission in the 73rd Highland Regiment in 1787.

INFANTRY OF THE LINE II

1. 14th Foot, 1812.
2. 69th Foot, 1812.
3. 32nd Foot, 1814–15.
4. 23rd Foot, 1812.
5. Officer, 9th Foot, 1813.
6. Private, Grenadier Company, 4th Foot, 1814.
7. The King's Colour, 69th Foot.

7
5
6
4
1
2
3

9
10
1
2
3
11
L.&F. FUNCKEN.

13
4
5
6
7
8

The Cavalry

One of the Duke of Wellington's first concerns was to ensure that the men were sensibly and practicably dressed and equipped. He himself, whenever possible, wore a plain uniform and a hat, small according to the fashions of the time. The cocked hat had been discontinued in the cavalry and was replaced by helmets or shakos. The greatest changes were made in the dress of the cavalry in 1811, when overalls, which were worn over the breeches and boots, were introduced. These were of various colours from grey to brown and of several patterns, some had a line of buttons down the side-seams and others had only a coloured stripe. These overalls were sometimes strapped and booted with leather, but there was another kind that was plain and fitted with four buttons and button-holes at the end of the leg, so that they could be more easily pulled over the boots. At this time, the sabretache was taken into general use.

Although the men were brave and well-mounted, Wellington was always somewhat dubious about the cavalry because of their lack of experience and the poor training of the officers. The Duke is reported to have said 'I did not like to see four British (squadrons) opposed to four French'.[14] For this reason, little use was made of the British cavalry during the Peninsular War. Nevertheless it must not be forgotten, the cavalry played an important part in the Battle of Salamanca. The Battle of Waterloo confirmed Welling-

14. *A History of the Peninsular War, 1807–1814* by Sir Charles W. C. Oman, Volume I, p. 119.

SCOTTISH REGIMENTS
(previous page)

1. Piper, 71st Foot, 1815.
2. Private, 79th Foot.
3. Officer, 42nd Foot, 1808.
4. Private, 92nd Foot.
5. Drummer, 92nd Foot, 1815.
6. Private, Light Infantry Company, 73rd Foot, 1812.
7. Sergeant, 71st Foot, 1808.
8. Sergeant, 79th Foot, 1815.
9. Private, 71st Foot, 1815.
10. Bugler, 71st Foot, 1815.
11. 1st Foot, 1815.
12. Private, Grenadier Company, 72nd Foot.
13. 71st Foot, 1815.

HUSSARS

1. 15th Hussars.
2. 7th Hussars.
3. 10th Hussars.
4. Officer, 15th Hussars.

4
3
2

ton's doubts about the cavalry. At Papelotte on 18 June 1815, the British cavalry under the command of the Earl of Uxbridge, attacked some retreating French infantry columns and a weak cavalry force. Encouraged by their initial success the cavalry, under Lord Edward Somerset and Sir William Ponsonby, disregarded the order to disengage and charged the French again who had re-formed by then. Even before they had reached the front rank of the enemy, a third of their number, 2,500 men, had been put out of action. This disobedience to orders cost Sir William Ponsonby his life.

The British cavalry was divided into light and heavy regiments. The former had curved swords, the latter straight ones; both with larger blades than those of the French army. Although they were heavy to handle, they inflicted severe wounds.

The Light Cavalry

The light cavalry consisted of the light dragoons and the hussars. The latter, of whom there were four regiments in 1811, had been converted from light dragoon regiments. They still retained their former names and numbers, the fact that they were hussars was indicated in the Army List only in brackets.

LIGHT DRAGOONS

1. 13th Light Dragoons.
2. 8th Light Dragoons.
3. 17th Light Dragoons.

2
3
1
F. FUNCKEN.

The hussars were dressed after the manner of the Hungarian hussars, with busby, dolman and pelisse. To complete the effect, they wore moustaches. Overalls were essential, as their tight white breeches did not stand up to the long rides in the summer dust and the winter mud. The busby which was more decorative than useful, replaced the shako.

The light dragoons' uniform was also changed, and their fur-crested helmet gave place to the shako. This change proved somewhat dangerous at first, because their shakos were very like those of the French, which resulted in their being fired upon by their own side. On service, the white breeches were replaced by blue-grey pantaloons.

HOUSEHOLD CAVALRY

1. Royal Horse Guards (The Blues).
2. 2nd Life Guards, 1810.
3. Officer, Life Guards, 1815.
4. Private, Life Guards, 1814.
5. Corporal, Life Guards.

Light Cavalry Regiments in 1815

	FACINGS	LACE
7th or The Queen's Own Regiment of Light Dragoons (Hussars)	White	Silver
8th or The King's Own Regiment of Light Dragoons (Hussars)	Scarlet	Gold
9th Regiment of Light Dragoons	Crimson	Gold
10th or The Prince of Wales's Own Royal Regiment of Light Dragoons (Hussars)	Crimson	Silver
11th Regiment of Light Dragoons	Buff	Silver
12th or The Prince of Wales's Regiment of Light Dragoons	Yellow	Silver
13th Regiment of Light Dragoons	Buff	Gold
14th or The Duchess of York's Own Regiment of Light Dragoons	Orange	Silver
15th or The King's Own Light Dragoons (Hussars)	Scarlet	Silver
16th or The Queen's Light Dragoons	Scarlet	Silver
17th Regiment of Light Dragoons	White	Silver
18th Regiment of Light Dragoons (Hussars)	White	Silver
19th Regiment of Light Dragoons	Yellow	Gold
20th Regiment of Light Dragoons	Orange	Gold
21st Regiment of Light Dragoons	Black	Silver
22nd Regiment of Light Dragoons	White	Gold
23rd Regiment of Light Dragoons	Crimson	Silver
24th Regiment of Light Dragoons	Light Grey	Gold
25th Regiment of Light Dragoons	Light Grey	Silver

5
4
1
2
3
L. & F. FUNCKEN.

The Heavy Cavalry

The heavy cavalry comprised the Life Guards, the Royal Horse Guards, the Dragoon Guards and the Dragoons. The cocked hat was replaced in 1811, by a helmet similar to that worn by the French cuirassiers and carabiniers. The Household Cavalry wore helmets with crests, and the Dragoon Guards and Dragoons ones with manes, except for the 2nd Dragoons who retained the bearskin cap.

The 5th (Royal Irish) Dragoons were disbanded for indiscipline in 1799, and, so, do not appear in the following table, which gives the facings and lace of the heavy cavalry:

DRAGOON GUARDS AND DRAGOONS

1. 2nd Dragoons.
2. 1st Royal Dragoons.
3. 1st King's Dragoon Guards.

	FACINGS	LACE
1st Regiment of Life Guards	Blue	Gold
2nd Regiment of Life Guards	Blue	Gold
The Royal Regiment of Life Guards	Scarlet	Gold
1st or The King's Regiment of Dragoon Guards	Blue	Gold
2nd or The Queen's Regiment of Dragoon Guards	Black	Silver
3rd or The Prince of Wales's Regiment of Dragoon Guards	White	Gold
4th or The Royal Irish Regiment of Dragoon Guards	Blue	Silver
5th or The Princess Charlotte of Wales's Regiment Dragoon Guards	Green	Gold
6th Regiment of Dragoon Guards	White	Silver
7th or The Princess Royal's Dragoon Guards	Black	Gold
1st or Royal Regiment of Dragoons	Blue	Gold
2nd or Royal North British Regiment of Dragoons	Blue	Gold
3rd or The King's Own Regiment of Dragoons	Blue	Gold
4th or The Queen's Own Regiment of Dragoons	Green	Silver
6th or The Inniskilling Regiment of Dragoons	Yellow	Silver

2
3
1

The Engineers and Volunteers

Engineers

At this time, the Engineers comprised the Corps of Royal Engineers who were all Officers, and the Royal Sappers and Miners, formerly the Corps of Military Artificers, who were Other Ranks and officered by the Royal Engineers. The Military Artificers were originally merely civilian employees, and it was not until 1786 that they were given a uniform. The Engineers often distinguished themselves during the Peninsular War. We illustrate their dress in 1813.

Volunteers

In addition to the Fencibles[15] and the Militia,[16] both of which were raised under the central Government, there were numerous volunteer organisations, of which the oldest and the only one still surviving is the Honourable Artillery Company of London. This body consisted not only of Artillery, but also of Light Horse, Infantry, and Rifles. The original Volunteers were raised in 'penny packets' throughout the country, usually on the basis of the Company and the parish. When the war broke out again after the Peace of Amiens, outside London the Volunteers were reorganised on a county basis in battalions of Local Militia.

15. The Fencibles, who only existed between 1794 and 1802, were regular troops with a liability for home service only, i.e. they only served in the British Isles.

16. The Militia, which was constituted in 1662 and not abolished until 1908, was the citizen force in which there was a general liability to serve. In practice, the men were called up by ballot. The officers held their commissions from the Lord Lieutenant for the County. Their liability was restricted to home service but many militiamen volunteered to serve with the regular forces during the Napoleonic Wars.

VOLUNTEERS AND ENGINEERS

1. Officer, Honourable Artillery Company.
2–4. Officers, London Volunteers, 1805.
5. Private, London Volunteers, 1805.
6. Private, Honourable Artillery Company.
7. Gunner, Honourable Artillery Company, 1804.
8. Officer, Royal Engineers, 1813.
9. Sergeant, Royal Sappers and Miners, 1813.
10. Sapper, Royal Sappers and Miners, 1813.

1
2
3
4
5
6
7
8
9
10

The Artillery

The British field artillery had guns of six different calibres. Highly mobile and well able to defend itself, the artillery was not greatly influenced by the ideas of the Iron Duke, who had no faith in artillery duels and preferred to use his guns to protect his infantry by bringing fire to bear on the enemy columns.

Shrapnel, a first-class invention that was to supplant all other types of ammunition for more than a century, appeared in 1784. Lieutenant Henry Shrapnel R.A. had perfected a projectile that burst in the air and showered the area with leaden balls.

Another invention, which originated in the Royal Navy, and was modified to suit land warfare in 1808, was the rocket. This weapon was developed by Major-General Sir William Congreve, and was made in six different calibres: 3, 6, 9, 12, 18, and 24 pounds. There was a special section of the artillery, the Rocket Troop, who operated the weapon. The rockets were discharged from a tripod and were fired by means of a flint-lock. Being much lighter and less cumbersome than the normal artillery, a team of only two to four men, according to the calibre, was required for each launcher. Rockets were used at Leipzig and at Waterloo. Although they had a good range (2,000 yards), they were not particularly accurate and they were really only useful for setting fire to buildings. After the Napoleonic wars, they fell into disuse.

ARTILLERY

1. Officer, Royal Horse Artillery, 1815.
2. Driver, Royal Horse Artillery, 1802.
3. Gunner, Royal Horse Artillery, 1812.
4. Gunner, Royal Artillery, 1814.
5. Rocket Troop, Royal Artillery, 1815.
6. 9 pounder gun, 1815.
7. 5.5-in Howitzer, 1815.
8. Gunner, Royal Artillery, 1815.
9. Gunner, Royal Horse Artillery, 1812.
10. Gunner, Royal Artillery.
11. Congreve Rocket Launcher in firing position, 1815.

11
5
10
9
6
7
8
1
2
3
4

The King's German Legion

During the wars of 1801 to 1806, Hanover was four times occupied; by the Prussians in 1801 and in 1805 and by the French in 1803 and in 1806. The state was finally dismembered by Napoleon who took the northern part for himself and gave the southern part to his brother Jerome, King of Westphalia.

A part of the Hanoverian army accepted service under their new masters, but a large number preferred to serve in the British Army, as their country had been closely linked with Britain since an earlier Elector of Hanover had succeeded to the British throne as King George I in 1714.

King George III charged Baron von der Decken with raising a corps of light infantry to be known as The King's Germans. Between 1803 and 1813, several thousand Hanoverians joined the 430 original recruits, so that a sizeable force of infantry, cavalry and artillery came into being in the end and was known as The King's German Legion.

This band of patriots fought in many campaigns, particularly in the Peninsular War, and gained the admiration of the British commanders under whom they served. They also played a large part in the Battle of Waterloo.

KING'S GERMAN LEGION

1–3. Officers, 1st, 2nd, and 3rd Hussars.
4. Horse Artillery, 1812.
5. Light Dragoon.
6. 1st Regiment, Light Infantry.
7. Foot Artillery, 1815.
8. Infantry of the Line.

4
5
6
1
2
3
8
L.&F.

THE PRUSSIAN ARMY

Frederick William III succeeded his father, a nephew of Frederick the Great, in 1797.[17] 'Old Fritz', who had little time for his nephew, had nevertheless taken him with him during the Seven Year's War. The future Frederick William II showed no promise, either as a soldier or as a politician. Having come to the throne, he took no interest in the education of his son, who was to become Frederick William III, and whose childhood was not very happy. This gave the son an inferiority complex that influenced him during the rest of his life.

Napoleon, with a characteristic shrewdness, summed him up as being 'as block-headed as a sergeant'. Perhaps not deserving quite so insulting a description, the King of Prussia was undoubtedly a weak character and politically inept. Frederick William III remained stubbornly neutral, hoping thereby to gain the good graces of Napoleon. This craven behaviour, however, only encouraged the Corsican to annex further territory and Frederick's hopes were dashed.

17. See *Arms and Uniforms II–18th Century to the Present Day*.

INFANTRY OF THE LINE I

1. Grenadier, 13th Regiment, 1805.
2. Private, 25th Regiment, 1806.
3. Grenadier, 15th Regiment, 1806.
4. Officer, 23rd Regiment, 1806.
5. Grenadier, 26th Regiment, 1806.
6. Private, 4th Regiment, 1807.

6
4
1
2
3

Napoleon, flushed with the victory of Austerlitz on 2 December 1805, stood out against the proposed confederation of states under the aegis of Prussia, and forced her to sign a military alliance with France. The outcome was that Frederick William III found himself compelled to annex Hanover, which was tantamount to declaring war on England, who described Prussia's action as 'contemptible servility and hateful brigandage'.

There is no doubt that these happenings increased the Prussians' dislike of the French. Frederick William, egged on by his wife, Louise of Mecklenburg-Strelitz, suddenly felt the urge to emulate his great-uncle and resolved to stand up to Napoleon. However, he also had the good sense to sign a secret treaty with Russia first of all. On 9 August 1806, a partial mobilization was ordered, and on 6 September the North Sea ports were opened to Britain. Finally, an ultimatum was sent to the Emperor demanding reparations and the evacuation of all French troops from German soil by 8 October.

'Marshal,' said Napoleon to the Prince of Neuchâtel (Marshal Berthier), when he received the communication, 'we have received a challenge for October the 8th, one that no Frenchman can refuse. Let us imagine that a beautiful queen wishes to be present, so let us be courteous and let us march straight for Saxony.'[18]

18. *Histoire de la Garde Impériale* by Marco de Saint-Hilaire.

INFANTRY OF THE LINE II

1. Sharpshooter, 40th Regiment, 1806.
2. Bandsman.
3. Private, 43rd Regiment, 1806.
4. Private, Light Infantry, 1806.
5. Officer, Battalion Company, Light Infantry, 1806.

4
5
2
1
3

As good as his word, Napoleon left Paris on 28 September and established his headquarters at Bamberg on 6 October 1806. An army of 166,000 with 234 guns was assembled there, and Napoleon issued the following proclamation, which we here reproduce verbatim:

"Soldiers! The order has already been given for your return to France. A triumphal entry awaits you in the capital. But before we sigh with relief, we must realise that new threats are growing behind the smiling mask of the alliance. Cries for war are to be heard in Berlin; for two months now we have been provoked. The same people, full of the same giddy ideas, are the ones now dominating Prussian politics.

'It is not Paris that they will burn; rather it will be their flags, which they reckon to raise in the capitals of our allies. They wish to throw us out of Saxony, and give it, by an underhand deal, its independence, in return for a number of its provinces; it is your laurels which they wish to tear up in front of you. They expect us to flee Germany on seeing their army. What idiots! They think it will be a thousand times easier to destroy our great capital than to corrupt children!

'Soldiers! Everyone of you that returns to France will return on the road of glory. Remember that all of you will be passing under triumphal arches!

INFANTRY I

1. 2nd Regiment, East Prussia, 1815.
2. Winter dress, 1812.
3. 3rd Regiment, Silesia.
4. Silesian Volunteers.
5–8. Officers, Non-Commissioned officer and Private, 1st Regiment of Guards.

1
2
3
4
5
6
7
8

'Then let us march, and show Prussia the mistake she has made in ignoring our warnings. Let us see how her army stands up to one proved in fourteen years fighting! Let us teach these soldiers that while it is easy to grow strong in a friendly nation, the anger of an incensed people can be worse than the storms of the sea!'

Incredibly, it was with these words that Napoleon captivated his men and urged them on.

The Prussians opposed the French with an army of 200,000, including Saxons and Hessians, all equally convinced of their superiority. Queen Louisa, the great patriot, rode beside her husband, wearing the uniform of Her Regiment of Dragoons. The Prussian Army was very smart and well-disciplined. The cavalry was well-mounted and the men were brave. The artillery enjoyed a high reputation. Unfortunately, they stuck, with a religious fervour, to the military theories of 'Old Fritz' which, while excellent at Rossbach and at Leuthen in 1757, were hopelessly out-of-date and worse than useless for dealing with Napoleon.

To command this army, the King of Prussia had dug out all the old generals of the Seven Years' War, such as the Duke of Brunswick (1735–1806), one of the greatest generals

INFANTRY II

1. Winter dress, 1815.
2. Officer, *Garde du Corps*, 1814.
3. General Officer, service dress, 1815.
4. Volunteer, East Prussia, 1814.
5. Silesian Militia, 1815.
6. Guards Bandsman, 1813.

6
1
2
3
4
5

in Europe, but now seventy-one years of age. Richard von Möllendorf (1724–1816), who had been a page to Frederick II and was now 82, rode with the grandson of his former master against the French. Gebhard von Blücher (1742–1819) was young by comparison, being only 64, but he had to wait until Waterloo when he was 72, before he had his revenge. A little younger still was the Prince of Hohenlohe-Ingelfingen (1746–1818), who was then 60 and a popular general, but his defeat at Jena on 14 October 1806 and his surrender at Prenzlau a fortnight later did much to undermine the morale of the Prussian people.

One of the King's cousins, Prince Louis of Prussia, who had been violently in favour of making war against France, was one of its first victims. He was killed in single combat with Sergeant Guindy, of the French 10th Hussars, whilst holding the bridge at Saalfeld on 10 October 1806.

The Prussian infantry had changed little since the death of Frederick II, and was dressed and equipped after the manner of the 18th century. This gave it a strange appearance alongside other armies. The cocked hat was decorated with pompoms and bound with a broad lace, the hair was worn in a queue and the coat was cut and faced as it had been during the Seven Years' War. Behind the left shoulder, there was a short strap that served to hold the brace of the cartridge-pouch. The grenadiers wore a special headdress which consisted of a small round flat cap with a large frontal edged with black fur.

CHASSEURS OF THE GUARD

1. 1809.
2. 1806.
3. 1813.
4. Officer, 1809.
5. 1814.

1
2
3
4
5

There were sixty regiments of infantry, including the foot guards. Some had French-sounding names, because, among the colonels, there were descendants of the Protestants who had chosen exile to escape the persecution of Louis XIV. The regiments were distinguished by colour of the collar, lapels, and cuffs, and by the shape of the buttonhole decorations and the spacing of the buttons.

The Infantry Regiments of Prussia and their distinguishing colours

NAME	COLOUR
1 Grafkulnhelm	Crimson
2 Rüchel	Salmon Pink
3 Renouard	Crimson, blue lapels
4 Kalkreuth	Saffron
5 Kleist	White
6 Grenadier-Garde	Red
7 Owstien	Lilac
8 Ruits	Red
9 Schenck	Red
10 Wedel	Pale Ochre
11 Schöning	Dark Grey
12 Braunschweigdels	Salmon Pink
13 Arnim	White
14 Besser	Salmon Pink
15 Leibgarde, 1st Batt.	Crimson
15 Regiment Garde	Crimson
16 Diericke	Salmon Pink
17 Treskow	White
18 Regiment des Königs	Lilac
19 Prince of Orange	Saffron
20 Prince L. Ferdinand	Red
21 Von Braunschweig	Red
22 Pirsch	Crimson
23 Winning	Lilac
24 Zenge	Crimson
25 von Möllendorf	Red
26 Alt-Larisch	Orange

LIGHT TROOPS

1. Fusiliers, Silesia, 1810.
2. Fusiliers, Silesia, 1812.
3. Chasseur, East Prussia, 1813.
4. Non-Commissioned officer, Chasseurs, East Prussia, 1808.
5. Cornet-player, Fusiliers, Silesia, 1814.

1
2
3
4
5
L. & F. FUNCKEN.

NAME	COLOUR
27 Tschammer	Crimson
28 Malschitzki	Pale Ochre
29 Treuenfels	Dark Grey
30 Borke	Pale Ochre
31 Prince Heinrich	Pale Olive
32 Hohenlohe	Pale Ochre
33 Alvensleben	White
34 Prince Ferdinand of Prussia	Crimson
35 Prince Heinrich of Prussia	Pale Olive
36 Puttkamer	White
37 Tschepe	Dark Grey
38 Pelchzrim	Red
39 Zastrow	White
40 Schimonsky	Lilac
41 Lettow	Crimson
42 Plötz	Dark Yellow
43 Strachwitz	Gold
44 Hagken	Pale Ochre
45 Zweiffel	Ochre
46 Thile	Black
47 Grawert	Ochre
48 Kurfürst von Hessen	Crimson
49 Müffling	White
50 Sanitz	Lilac
51 Kauffberg	Pale Green
52 Reinhart	Red
53 Jung-Larisch	Pale Green
54 Natzmer	Pale Ochre
55 Marstein	Pale Ochre
56 Taventzien	Red
57 Grevenitz	Rose Pink
58 Courbière	Pale Green
59 Wartensleben	White
60 Chlebowsky	Yellow

The Cavalry

The heavy cavalry, the cuirassiers, wore a white, close-fitting uniform, also very out-of-date in style. The distin-

HUSSARS I

1. Regiment von Prittwitz, 1806.
2. Regiment von Pietz, 1806.
3. Regiment Prinz Eugen von Württemberg, 1807.
4. Regiment von Rudorff, 1807.

3
4
2
1

guishing colours included pale blue, dark blue, red and violet. The 2nd Cuirassiers wore a yellow uniform.

The light cavalry was composed of hussars, whose dress was similar to that of the hussars of other armies. The Regiment von Prittwitz wore shakos with the Death's-Head badge.

This colourful army set forth in three columns and crossed the Elbe at Dresden and at Magdeburg. It was a grave error in that the army advanced on too broad a front, the three columns were each separated by 47 miles. Napoleon, for his part, advanced to meet them on a front of barely 37 miles, so that his three columns were less than 20 miles apart.

Disorganised after the first encounter, the Prussians tried to restore their position, but in so doing they let Napoleon cut them off from Silesia where the Russians should have come to their help under the secret pact. The final clash came on 14 October 1806, when two battles, Auerstädt and Jena, were fought at the same time. At the former, Davout with 28,700 men defeated the King of Prussia and the Duke of Brunswick with 60,500 men, and the Duke was mortally wounded. At the cost of one-third of their own strength, the French killed or wounded 10,000 Prussians, took 3,000 prisoners and captured 115 guns. At Jena, with 56,000 men, Napoleon destroyed the forces of von Hohenlohe and of von Rüchel, 72,000 Prussians and Saxons, killing or wounding

HUSSARS II

1. Non-Commissioned officer, Brandenburg Hussars.
2. Officer, 1st Regiment Leibhusaren.
3. 1st Silesian Hussars, 1815.
4. Pomeranian Hussars, 1810.
5. Non-Commissioned officer, 2nd Silesian Hussars, 1809.

3
4
5
1
2

12,000, taking 15,000 prisoners and capturing 30 colours and 200 guns.

Despite their undoubted courage, the Prussians had experienced a military catastrophe. The remnants of the army, rallied by Hohenlohe, attempted to join the Russian army on the other side of the Oder. After an exhausting march lasting five days, the 70,000 survivors had covered 125 miles of almost impossible side-tracks and took refuge in Magdeburg. The 6,000 who got away from Auerstädt were less fortunate, for they were forced to surrender at Erfurt on 15 October. Napoleon was determined that not a single Prussian regiment should escape, and pursued the fugitives relentlessly. Hohenlohe, realising the danger, divided his forces in two and succeeded in getting 45,000 men within fifty miles of the Oder. However, Lasalle's hussars got there first and, although there were less than 700 of them, they succeeded in routing the Prussians and driving them into the ancient city of Prenzlau where they surrendered on 28 October.

Bit by bit, the Prussian army was rounded up. The last to admit defeat was Blücher who tried to save his men by marching towards the Baltic. He struggled on until 7 November when he surrendered 15,000 men and fifteen colours. On the following day, Magdeburg fell, thus completing the destruction of Frederick William III's army. In thirty-nine days, Napoleon had taken 140,000 prisoners and 250 colours.

CUIRASSIERS I

1. Officer, Regiment Quitzow, 1806.
2. Private, Regiment von Beeren, 1806.

2
1

The outcome of the war brought the Prussian people near to despair, but it also served to show up some of the shortcomings of the army. Reforms, both social and military, were introduced and every effort was made to awake a spirit of patriotism and to foster a movement towards liberty. In 1809, Frederick William founded the University of Berlin, and Wilhelm von Humboldt was installed as its head.

Compelled to side with France in the Russian campaign, the Prussian army formed the rearguard under Alexander Macdonald (Marshal, Duke of Tarento, 1765–1840). The Prussian commander, Count Hans York von Wartenburg (1759–1830), signed an independent treaty of neutrality with the Russians on 28 February 1813 and withdrew his forces. Frederick William first of all accused his general of insubordination and then, realising that he could make capital out of it, decided to throw in his lot with the patriots who were struggling against the French. One of the leaders of the resistance after 1808 was Count Neidhardt von Gneisenau (1760–1831), who had been a company commander at Jena. Gneisenau realised that the old mercenary army had to be replaced by a citizen army made up of men of liberal ideas and led by highly professional officers, rather than by a King who had too often shown his incapacity.

The Infantry

The new army was conscripted after the pattern of the armies of Napoleon, and was organised in army corps, each made up of infantry, cavalry and artillery. Although modelled on French lines, the Prussian army lacked the driving

CUIRASSIERS II

1. Brandenburg Regiment, 1813.
2. Cossack, *Garde du Corps*, 1814.
3. Private, *Garde du Corps*.

1
2
3

force that was so necessary. Too often, there was a tendency for commanders to take independent action which was frequently haphazard and timid.

The uniforms worn at Jena had gone. The hat was replaced by the shako and the new infantry coatee had short skirts. The grey greatcoats were carried *en banderole*. Regiments were no longer known by the names of their Colonels for the time being, but by territorial names; Silesia, Pomerania, East Prussia, West Prussia and so on. From 1808, each infantry regiment was composed of two line battalions and one light infantry battalion. The grenadiers were formed in independent battalions. In 1810, an extra strap was added to the equipment. This went across the chest and gave the Prussian soldier a characteristic appearance. The light infantry were dressed in green and carried short rifled carbines, which were light and very accurate.

Through lack of experience, the Prussian infantry were never able to adapt themselves to Wellington's tactics for dealing with the French columns.[19] For the same reason, the cavalry of the Army of Liberation was, likewise, no match for the French cuirassiers, but they proved themselves of value in a reconnaissance role.

The Prussian cuirassiers wore a white coatee, known as a *Kollet*. On service, they wore a *Litewka*, a jacket of Lithuanian origin. The same applied to the dragoons. The hussars retained their characteristic dress. Beside them, there were

19. See pages 92 to 105.

CHASSEURS À CHEVAL AND HUSSARS

1. 1st Regiment Leibhusaren, 1813–14.
2. Chasseur, Guard Hussars, 1813.
3. Non-Commissioned officer, Dragoons.
4. Chasseur, 1st Silesian Hussars.

5, 6. Shakos.

7. Sabretache and Swords.

8, 9. Trumpets, Hussars and Chasseurs.

10,11. Pistol and Carbine, Hussars.

6
7
1
2
3
4
8
9
10
11

the volunteer mounted riflemen who wore a green uniform. On service, all the cavalry wore overalls.

The artillery was composed of 3 pounders, 6 pounders and 12 pounders and, modelled on French lines, was of a high standard. All the same, like the other arms of the service, it lacked experience.

For all of this, however, the Prussian army played an important part in the campaigns of the closing days of the Empire. The indefatigable Blücher, despite the numerous defeats, knew how to encourage his men as their enthusiasm and their patriotic fervour were beginning to cool, whatever may have been written to the contrary. The 'extraordinary enthusiasm' of the Prussian people for the liberation movement in 1813 had only produced 22,000 volunteers in three months, and it became necessary to call upon the 120,000 *Landwehr* (militia) to bring the army up to strength for the autumn campaign.

The Prussian army underwent many changes, especially during the French campaign in 1814, where Napoleon displayed his military genius to its utmost, but Blücher never let himself be discouraged and fought on until Waterloo.

The Prussian crown gained nothing from the final victory, and, in any case, Queen Louisa never knew of it as she died in 1810. Her husband continued to annoy his people who eventually rose in revolt in 1830, and he died, forgotten, on 7 June 1840. No one has ever come forward to write the life of Old Fritz's great-nephew.

ARTILLERY

1. Gunner, Foot Artillery, 1808.
2, 3. Gunners, Foot Artillery, 1815.
4. Pioneer, 1813.
5. Field Officer, Horse Artillery, 1815.
6. Non-Commissioned officer, Horse Artillery, 1815.

5
6
2
4
1
3

THE SPANISH ARMY

The French had reckoned on taking Spain in their stride. Accordingly, Napoleon only sent a force of 35,000 experienced men and 75,000 recruits to occupy the country. Having forced the abdication of Charles IV and having deposed Ferdinand VII, Napoleon put his brother Joseph on the throne of Spain.

The uprising in Madrid on 2 May 1808 took the French, who were attacked and massacred in the streets, by surprise. The Spanish army took no part, only the civil population who seized 10,000 muskets from the arsenal. Murat called out his troops and order was restored, but only after 2,000 rioters had been killed by the bayonet and hundreds of others by the sabres of the cavalry. Merciless repression followed. The artist, Goya, recorded the terrible results.

Although it had been put down in Madrid, the revolt spread throughout Spain. In June 1808, 5,000 French were driven out of Saragossa, which had a population of only 40,000, and the famous siege commenced. After breaching the walls, the French soldiers had to re-take the town, house by house. Between 4 and 14 August, only four houses fell which gives some idea of the determination of the defenders who were nearly all civilians. At Baylen, things went badly too, and a considerable French force was forced to surrender on 1 July 1808.

SPANISH CAVALRY

1. Cavalry of the Line, 1805.
2. Dragoons, 1805.
3. Horse Grenadiers, 1808.
4. Dragoons, 1808.
5. Lancers, 1810–11.
6. Cuirassiers, 1810–11.

1
2
3
4
5
6
& F. FUNCKEN.

Having decided to take matters in hand himself, Napoleon entered Spain at the head of an army of eight corps and the *Garde Impériale*, some 175,000 hardened men. The Spanish opposed him with 120,000 men under Palafox, Castanos and Benito San Juan. This army had just undergone extensive changes, both in organisation and in dress. Under Philip V (the grandson of Louis XIV), who was crowned King of Spain in 1700, the uniforms had been of French style.

One of the most famous regiments of the time were the Walloon Guards which had been raised in Belgium in 1702 for service under the young King. Over the years, they had recruited an increasing number of Spaniards, but even in Napoleon's day, there were quite a number of Belgian officers in the Spanish army, men such as Clément de Saint-Marcq who commanded the Army of Valencia and Aragon, the Baron de Warsage who organised a battalion of volunteers from among the students in the defence of Saragossa where he was killed, and the Marquis de Coupigny-Lignereuil who commanded the 2nd Division of the Army of Andalusia at the battles of Menjivar and Baylen.

The most popular of the Spanish generals was José de Palafox y Melzit, who symbolised the resistance to the Spanish, and led the uprising in Aragon in 1808. He was born in Aragon in 1780 and died in Madrid in 1847.

After 1808, the Spanish uniforms became English in style, often being identical, except for the colour. The explanation

SPANISH AND PORTUGUESE INFANTRY

1. Patria Regiment, 1808.
2. Officer, Santa Feé Regiment, 1808
3. Muerte Regiment, 1808.
4. Infantry of the Line, 1805.
5. Fernando VII Regiment, 1808.
6. Victoria Regiment, 1808.
7. Valencia Light Infantry.
8. Light Infantry, 1805.
9–10. Portuguese Grenadier and Chasseur.

9
10
8
7
1
2
3
4
5
6

was that the British had found in the Spanish insurrection an excuse for landing on the continent, even though they were officially at war with Spain. Having landed in Portugal, the expeditionary force likewise influenced the uniform of that country, and their infantry of the line, their *cacadores* (rifles), and their *atiradores* (light infantry) all adopted the British shako. Portuguese uniforms were usually brown, and the Spanish infantry of the line wore blue.

Some Spanish regiments commemorated the War of Independence by their names; thus Patria, Santa Fe, Victoria, Meurte and Fernando VII. Their musket were similar to the French, except for the lock. The guerillas played an important part in this bitter war. The worst attrocities were committed by the populace who set upon stragglers and even the wounded and prisoners.

The magnificent example of Spain, who had dared to oppose Napoleon, awoke the patriotism of many other peoples who, till then, had submitted. Among them, there were the Tyroleans under Andreas Hofer who, in 1809, refused to lay down their arms when Austria made peace.

Scarcely had Napoleon restored order in Spain, when the news reached him at Astorga of the treachery of Talleyrand[20] and Fouché.[21] Napoleon left Spain and returned to Paris at full speed to open up a new front in Europe.

20. Charles-Maurice de Talleyrand-Perigord (1754–1838).

21. Joseph Fouché, Duke of Otranto (1759–1820).

SPANISH INFANTRY, 1812

1. Grenadier.
2. Officer, Chasseurs.
3. Light Infantry.
4. Fusilier.
5. Chasseur.

1
2
3
4
5

Pictorial Glossary

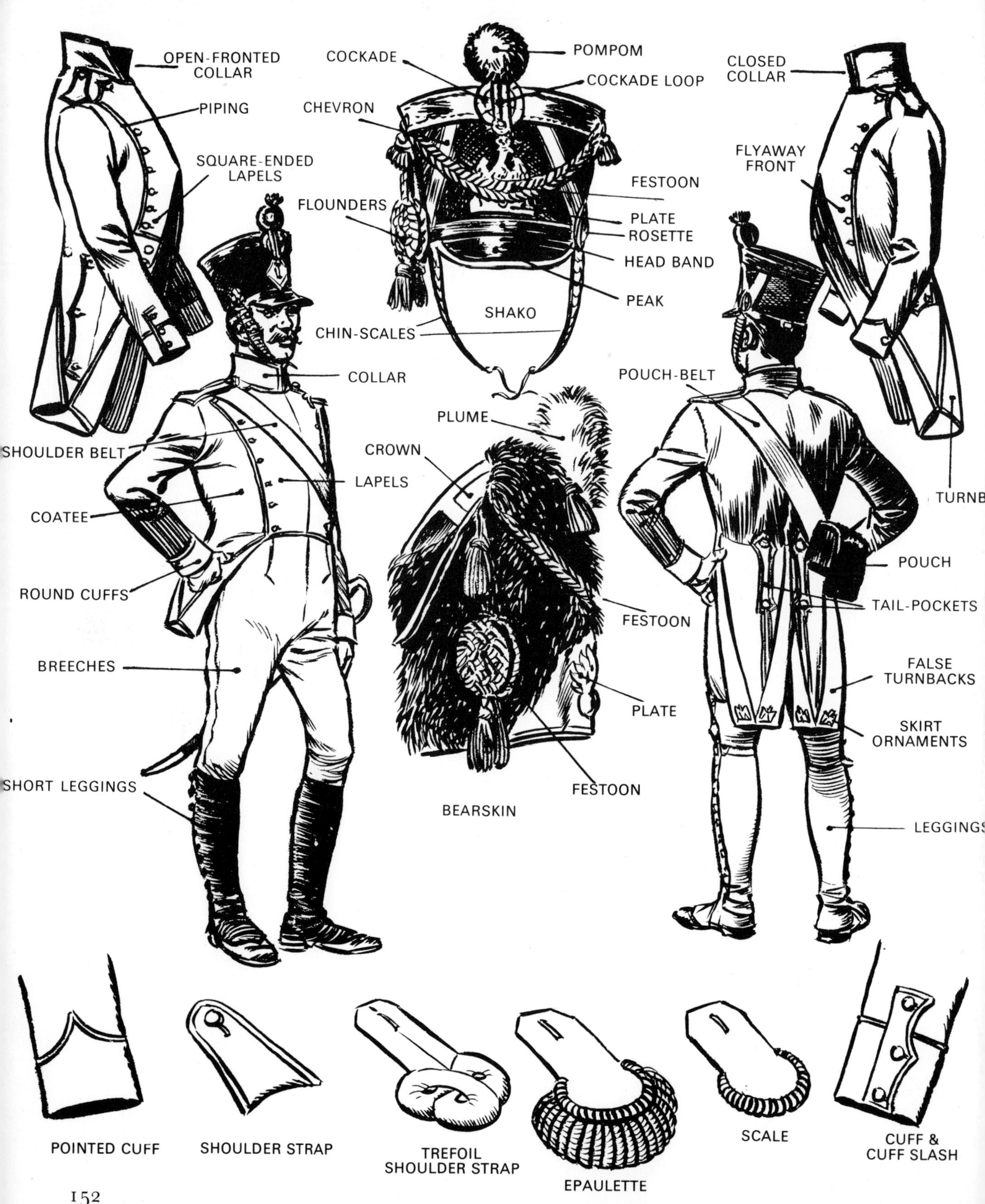
OPEN-FRONTED COLLAR
PIPING
SQUARE-ENDED LAPELS
COCKADE
POMPOM
COCKADE LOOP
CHEVRON
CLOSED COLLAR
FLYAWAY FRONT
FESTOON
FLOUNDERS
PLATE
ROSETTE
HEAD BAND
PEAK
SHAKO
CHIN-SCALES
COLLAR
POUCH-BELT
PLUME
SHOULDER BELT
CROWN
LAPELS
TURNB
COATEE
POUCH
ROUND CUFFS
TAIL-POCKETS
FESTOON
BREECHES
FALSE TURNBACKS
PLATE
SKIRT ORNAMENTS
SHORT LEGGINGS
FESTOON
BEARSKIN
LEGGINGS
POINTED CUFF
SHOULDER STRAP
TREFOIL SHOULDER STRAP
EPAULETTE
SCALE
CUFF & CUFF SLASH

SQUARE VALISE
SADDLE COVER
ROUND VALISE
LSTER-CAP
SADDLECOVER
PLUME
TUFT
CREST
FRONT OF CREST
SHELL
MANE
TURBAN
BUSBY
BUSBY-BAG
ROSETTE
SIDE-PLAITS
PEAK
QUEUE OR PIGTAIL
DOLMAN OR JACKET
CHIN-SCALES
PELISSE
VALISE
SHABRAQUE
SABRETACHE
CAVALRY BOOTS
POCKETS
HORIZONTAL
CUFFS
VERTICAL
ARD-OPENING
DOWNWARD-OPENING
L. et F. FUNCKEN. 68

Index

L. & F. FUNCKEN.